YOU CAN'T PUT GOD IN A BOX

YOU CAN'T PUT GOD IN A BOX

Thoughtful Spirituality in a Rational Age

Kelly Besecke

OXFORD
UNIVERSITY PRESS

OXFORD
UNIVERSITY PRESS

Oxford University Press is a department of the University of Oxford.
It furthers the University's objective of excellence in research, scholarship,
and education by publishing worldwide.

Oxford New York
Auckland Cape Town Dar es Salaam Hong Kong Karachi
Kuala Lumpur Madrid Melbourne Mexico City Nairobi
New Delhi Shanghai Taipei Toronto

With offices in
Argentina Austria Brazil Chile Czech Republic France Greece
Guatemala Hungary Italy Japan Poland Portugal Singapore
South Korea Switzerland Thailand Turkey Ukraine Vietnam

Oxford is a registered trade mark of Oxford University Press
in the UK and certain other countries.

Published in the United States of America by
Oxford University Press
198 Madison Avenue, New York, NY 10016

Library of Congress Cataloging-in-Publication Data
Besecke, Kelly, 1970–
   You can't put god in a box : thoughtful spirituality in a rational age / Kelly Besecke.
       p.   cm.
   Includes bibliographical references and index.
   ISBN 978–0–19–993094–4 (pbk. : alk. paper) — ISBN 978–0–19–993092–0 (hardcover : alk.
paper) — ISBN 978–0–19–993093–7 (ebook) 1. Faith and reason. 2. Religion—Philosophy.
3. Reason. I. Title.
   BL51.B544 2014
   204—dc23
                            2013011617

9 8 7 6 5 4 3 2 1

Printed in the United States of America on acid-free paper

In memory of

David Lyons, Cecil Findley, Wayne Teasdale, and Ron Miller.

Your words live on.

CONTENTS

ACKNOWLEDGMENTS

This book began its life in 1997, so I have more than fifteen years' worth of gratitude to express. I'll start at the beginning: Dan Prince gave me the Joseph Campbell tapes that sparked my imagination and led me to this project. Harmony Voorhies Tucker was the first person I talked with about these ideas, on the best road trip I've ever taken. Dan, Harmony, and I had been students together at Carleton College, and as the saying goes, I am a part of Carleton and Carleton is a part of me. My Carleton friends are still as amazing as they ever were. They've given me support, cheerleading, and suggestions as I've transformed what was a dissertation into a book. I'm especially grateful for Kathy Richards, Dan Simons, Kim Betz, Lory Hess, Catherine Dietz Spencer, and Gillie English Bishop. My professors at Carleton taught me to think sociologically and culturally; I am grateful for Nader Saiedi, Jim Fisher, John Ramsay, and Beverly Nagel.

Lyn Macgregor helped with the book's title and a variety of other titles through the years. Lyn, Tona Williams, Rebecca Krantz, Rachel Dwyer, Greta Krippner, and Susan Munkres were the graduate school cohorts who read chapters and helped sort out ideas in the coffee shops, parks, and neighborhoods of Madison, Wisconsin. Nina Eliasoph, Phil Gorski, Pam Oliver, and Jerry Marwell provided support and suggestions when I was a student and they were my professors at the University of Wisconsin.

Wade Clark Roof coined the term *reflexive spirituality*. His talk on this topic at the 1999 American Sociological Association meetings left me more animated than I have ever felt at an academic conference. His book *Spiritual Marketplace* is a treasure trove. Every time I think I've had an original idea, I find that he wrote about it there first. I'm also grateful for Thomas Luckmann's *The Invisible Religion*, Robert Bellah's *Beyond Belief*, and the writings of Victor Turner, Paul Ricoeur, and Joseph Campbell for making reflexive spirituality come alive and fall into place at the same time.

I owe some of the most important boons of my career to Nancy Ammerman. An early supporter of my work, she has gone out of her way to bring me and my ideas into the community of scholars of religion. She played a key part in my receiving a Louisville Institute Dissertation Fellowship and in bringing my work to the attention of Theo Calderara at Oxford University Press. I'm grateful to the Louisville Institute for making it possible to devote a full year to writing the first draft of this book, the dissertation. I'm grateful to Theo for bringing me on board at OUP and making my dream of this book come true.

The book has been a financial sacrifice. I'm grateful to the University of Wisconsin Department of Sociology for several small research and travel grants and for employing me as a teacher to support my research. Members of my family, the federal student loan program, my clients at Bookmark Editing, and the advice of Leslie Cunningham have all helped make the book financially possible.

Between finishing the dissertation and beginning the book, I worked as a professor at Colorado College and Kenyon College. I'm grateful to my students, especially the students in my Meaning in Modern Society seminars, for their energy, ideas, and feedback, and for the opportunity to explain these ideas in new ways. Special thanks to Hayden Schortman, who read more of my work than any student should ever have to do. At Kenyon, Allison Hurst, Anna Sun, and Jennifer Johnson read and commented on early outlines and chapter sections. And for their enthusiasm and support, I thank Jeff Livesay, Gail Murphy-Geiss, and Margi Duncombe at Colorado College and Jan Thomas at Kenyon.

I'm grateful for my family, especially Leslie Besecke, Anish Chatterjee, Alyson Chatterjee, Julia Chatterjee, Evan Chatterjee, and Ann Asel. A special shout-out goes to my niece Alyson, who played an instrumental role in this book when she was a baby. I was her nanny for six months, and living with her made it possible for me to study one of my primary field sites, Common Ground. My nieces and nephew are the coolest kids around.

My friends in Austin have been an integral part of the journey from dissertation to book and from professor to writer. Here's to the posse: Eileen Schrandt, Erika Frahm, Colleen Flynn, Angela Kizzee, and Jeanel Walker. Thanks also to the people who've participated in my Facebook author page. I'm astounded that not all of you are people who were already my friends. I'm grateful for both the old friends and those who have come into my life because of my writing.

My favorite parks and musicians have inspired my thinking. Many an idea was gestated in the Baraboo Hills and the Wisconsin state parks. And I'm grateful for the songwriters whose lyrics I quote: Chris Cunningham and Johnny Hermanson of Storyhill, Stuart Davis, and Peter Mayer. I hope you all check out them out at storyhill.com, stuartdavis.com, and petermayer.net.

Jamie Ridler and the community of creative women that she has built have been a huge support. I'm grateful for the Creative Dream Journalers, including especially Kim LeClair, Valarie Budayr, Glenda Miles, Alli Vee, Ginny Lennox, and Helen Yee.

Bill Minutaglio taught a very helpful class on writing nonfiction book proposals through the Writers' League of Texas. That class gave me my writing group in Austin: David Steinman, Earl Russell, Brenda Schoolfield, Jean Germain, Howard Hatfield, and Betty Duff gave excellent feedback on the book proposal and a variety of book summaries.

Finally, I come to the people who can't be thanked enough. The people this book is about—reflexive spiritualists—are lodged in my heart. I continue to be inspired by the people of First United Methodist Church, Common Ground, the Spirituality at Work movement, and everyone else whose words make this book.

My parents, Walt and Penny Besecke, have been with me throughout this journey, supporting me in its challenges and celebrating my accomplishments with a zeal that lifts me up in every moment. Since 1997, I've been anticipating the moment when I can hand my parents a copy of my book. No one will be prouder. Mom and Dad, I love you.

A writer is very lucky if she finds people to talk with about her ideas—people who are interested in the topics she writes about and can help her think things through. A writer is also very lucky if she comes across people who believe in and support her as a human being while she undertakes a big, long-term project with an uncertain outcome. It's an amazing experience to meet with people who are both of these things at the same time—people who love both the ideas and the person. I've been so lucky as to meet two people like this who have been integral to the two different phases of the book's development.

Colleen Moore has been my best friend as I've transformed my dissertation into a book proposal and a book. She is a beautiful writer herself, and she is an educated seeker. She read the proposal and the manuscript, gave great feedback on both, and suggested several chapter titles. She talked with me about reflexive spirituality, religion and spirituality in general, money, writing, the meaning of life, and every other thing as we sat on my purple couch, at her kitchen table, at Mueller Park, and in the restaurants, coffee shops, and bookstores of Austin, Texas. She spun me around by telling me that my book mattered for people other than myself—that she couldn't wait to read it—that it wasn't just my own myopic vision, but something that other people might value.

Paul Lichterman was my dissertation adviser at the University of Wisconsin. Paul is a brilliant sociologist who loves an interesting idea. His careful analytical style kept me intellectually honest. He formed my thinking about culture, participant observation, and the relationship between field work and theory. It's hard work to truly get inside another person's developing ideas, and even harder to do that without taking the project over, but Paul consistently managed that balance. It took a good two years to clearly articulate what this thing was that I wanted to study for my dissertation, and Paul handled that delicate gestation time with grace, respect, and integrity. He responded to my vague statements of the topic by continually affirming that I was on to something good and patiently helping me figure out how to move forward. Ten years after finishing the dissertation, I remain enormously grateful for his commitment to me and to the development of my ideas.

YOU CAN'T PUT GOD IN A BOX

PREFACE: MEANING, MIND, AND RELIGION IN TWO LIVES

This book began with my own quest for meaning. In 1997, I had been a graduate student for four years. Graduate school is intense for everyone, but people's specific experiences vary. For me, the experience had been alienating—all mind, no soul. Those four years narrowed me down to a brain, an analyzer, walking around in an intellect-only world. There was no zest in my life, no sparkle or spirit. I stopped attending to the needs of my body, heart, and soul. My relationships with other people were intellectual, and impersonal.

Many years later, I read *Eat, Pray, Love* and was delighted by Elizabeth Gilbert's description of herself as "the planet's most affectionate life form." Her relationship with an emotionally unavailable man was killing her from the inside.

I am perhaps the planet's most personal life form. My enthusiasm for genuine, heartfelt, open, deeply felt connection encompasses not only people and dogs, but also trees, bricks, clouds, and bodies of water. Once I cut into a tomato with visible veins and was racked by guilt, conscious of killing a living thing (with *veins*) just to satisfy my own selfish culinary desires. Other times I am a vulture, thriving on others' pain because when people are vulnerable, then they'll really open up. I am every stereotype—a tree-hugging bleeding heart liberal idealist who's "too sensitive." I stop and smell *all* the roses.

Training myself to proceed through life as a disembodied brain was not the kindest thing I could have done for myself. And the truth is, it never really took. I made a good go of it, though, through the coursework, master's thesis, and preliminary exams required by my PhD program, so that four years later I could take a break to ponder possible topics for the final requirement, the dissertation. Then my best friend from college called. She had just finished her own graduate program and was celebrating by taking a month-long road trip across the Midwest and Rocky Mountains to see friends, family, and national parks. Did I want to come along?

One of our first stops was a friend's cabin on Ottertail Lake in upstate Minnesota. He said, "I have the perfect thing for you guys to listen to on your road trip," and handed us six cassettes on which he had crossed out assorted '80s heavy metal titles and written in "Joseph Campbell and the Power of Myth, 1–6."

Joseph Campbell blew my mind. In this classic series of interviews with Bill Moyers, Campbell made myth and religion come alive by unpacking their potential to speak to the depths of people's inner and outer lives. Campbell spoke of the heroism of ordinary life, the mystery in which we are all always participating, and the rapture of feeling truly alive. He spoke of the god within each individual, the struggle for authenticity, and the achievement of becoming our true selves. Campbell interpreted religious stories and myths as metaphors that meet us in the terms of our ordinary experience but point us to realities that lie beyond ordinary experience. Religion, he said, is meant to help people experience sacredness, and the gods of religion are masks of divinity that reflect the ultimate mystery—the "God beyond God."

Coming as they did after a four-year spiritual drought, those interviews with Bill Moyers seemed to open up for me a world of significance, of transcendent meaning, of "something more"—more than just the practical world of the dominant culture, and more than just the intellectual world of academia. I felt shot through with the vertical dimension of life, with a deep resonance between each moment and the infinite. I saw layers of meaning unfolding like the layers of an onion. I understood the eternal moment. It's not that different from the pregnant pause. There were connections between my life and eternity, between my stories and religious stories, my ordinary experience and mystical experience.

This was what I wanted to study for my dissertation. The only trouble was, what *was* "this"? In those days, the word *spirituality*, as in "I'm not religious but I'm spiritual," had not yet become popular. Looking back, however, what I was hearing in those Joseph Campbell interviews had everything to do with spirituality—a sense of meaning, a felt connection to "something more," a depth of experience, a profound sense of orientation to the movements of life. But this was a particular kind of spirituality, one that somehow spoke deeply to my ambivalent relationship to academia and the life of the mind.

On one hand, the kind of spirituality hinted at in *The Power of Myth* promised a sparkle and a personal depth that my academic life was missing. On the other hand, this spirituality took full advantage of the resources of academia, using scholarship in a way I had never heard it used before. Campbell drew on the work of psychologists, anthropologists, philosophers, and literary icons, including Sigmund Freud, Carl Jung, Abraham Maslow, Friedrich Nietzsche, Arthur Schopenhauer, James Frazer, and James Joyce. More significantly, Campbell used the methods of scholarship: systematic comparison and textual analysis. But he used these methods and resources—the methods and resources of systematic reason—to point to realities that ultimately lay beyond the world of reason. It was this intersection, this creative combination of reason and spirit, that attracted me.

Ultimately, I came to identify this kind of spirituality with what sociologist Wade Clark Roof has called *reflexive spirituality*. *Reflexive* here has more to do with *reflection* than with *reflex* and describes a habit of "stepping back" mentally from one's own perspective to reflect on it objectively. Reflexive spirituality is a thoughtful, deliberate, open approach to cultivating religious meaning. When I am practicing a reflexive spirituality, I am constantly reflecting on my own spiritual perspective in light of other possible spiritual perspectives. I'm making a point of finding out about the many religious symbols and spiritual ideas that are out there in the world, and I'm thoughtfully considering them in relation to my own spiritual ideas and experiences. When I am practicing a reflexive spirituality, I'm making a habit of holding my own spirituality out at arm's length to consider it objectively, and I'm constantly searching out new religious ideas, new sources of wisdom, new images, stories, and rituals, with the design of incorporating them critically into my own spiritual outlook.

This was the kind of spirituality I heard in *The Power of Myth*—one that respected both reason and that which lies beyond reason, one that approached religion as a resource for the cultivation of wisdom rather than as a set of pat answers. I knew that this kind of spirituality was not unique to Joseph Campbell, but rather that Campbell must be only part of a more broad-based spiritual subculture. After all, the trade paperback of *The Power of Myth* was a bestseller, and the videos were replayed endlessly on public television ten years after their original airing. Joseph Campbell had a big audience—but what else was this audience doing spiritually? I wanted to find out. I wanted to understand this spiritual subculture and its way of engaging reason, religion, and meaning. So I embarked on a five-year study of reflexive spirituality. I visited churches and adult education centers, attended lectures and listened to radio interviews with book authors, and joined groups about spirituality at work, interfaith education, and meditation. Everywhere I went, I listened to how people talked about meaning, religion, and reason—how people practiced reflexive spirituality. It was a spiritual quest and an intellectual quest, and what it meant for me—the part that reflexive spirituality and this book would play in my personal story—was crystallized midway through my research, in the summer of 2000.

It was early evening, and I was sitting with members of an interfaith discussion group at one of their weekly meetings. The group had invited Professor Cohen, chair of the University of Wisconsin's brand-new program in religious studies, to speak about potential connections between the university and the group's own agenda for interfaith education. Professor Cohen was excited about the new program and described for the group the recently approved requirements for the religious studies major. He went over the first four quickly—these were typical of requirements for a major in any liberal arts discipline:

1. Examine a variety of the world's religious traditions.
2. Understand at least one tradition in depth.
3. Understand different methodological approaches to religion.
4. Assess scholarly literatures on religion, conduct original research into the subject, and present conclusions clearly in speech and writing.

He lingered on requirement number five:

5. Become familiar with manifestations of religious awe in such things as texts, rituals, social institutions, and personal expression.

"I pushed for this one," he said. "My argument was that students can't really understand religion if they don't understand something about religious awe."

From Professor Cohen's point of view, an "awe" requirement was daring. *Awe.* From a scholarly point of view, it was too hard to pin down—too subjective, too emotional, too fuzzy, too *irrational.* The first four requirements—those were easier to specify and evaluate objectively. But who's to say what demonstrates "awe" and what doesn't?

After all, no other academic department had a requirement anything like it. The sociology department taught students to think analytically about society, but it didn't ask them to become familiar with manifestations of human compassion. The philosophy department didn't require familiarity with manifestations of wisdom. Even art history didn't require familiarity with manifestations of aesthetic arrest, of people overwhelmed by beauty. Universities just didn't do those things. Universities were about systematic observation, logic, and reason—not subjective inspiration. So to insist that to truly understand religion, students must understand—or at least learn about—religious awe seemed like a groundbreaking move.

Professor Cohen's talk ended, and after a little conversation, he left the group members to continue their meeting. Looking around, I was surprised to see them rolling their eyes and giggling, and even more surprised to find out why. "What did you think of his requirements?" one asked, with smiling eyes and raised eyebrows. "'Oh yeah, that awe thing,'" another said. "Yeah, that thing that's the only thing that really matters—better just tack that on at the end." "That awe thing," someone else repeated, shaking his head. "Leave it to academia."

I realized that when this group, formed around a deep interest in the spiritual wisdom of the world's religions, saw the "awe" requirement, they didn't see the groundbreaking move of a scholar defying the conventions of academia. Instead, they saw academia's continued—and to their eyes great—limitations. They saw the most important thing about religion marginalized—considered as an afterthought, tacked on to the end of a list that emphasized numbers and techniques at the expense of any of the heart, the substance, of religious life.

Academia versus spirituality, I thought. Which group did I belong to—the reasonable, or the inspired? Was I a logical thinker, analytic, systematic, and objective? Or was I a spiritual person, in touch with the essence of what really matters?

Like most things, this book is personal to me. For me, it's been a project of personal integrity. Reflexive spirituality relies on both reason and imagination, both systematic observation and intuitive leaps of faith, both logical analysis and mystical experience, both objective understanding and subjective awe. So do I. Reflexive spirituality refuses to compromise between rationality and spirituality, instead integrating the two by putting them in creative dialogue with each other. It emerges from this dialogue with new possibilities for meaning, vitality, wisdom, and authenticity. And so, in the end, did I.

*   *   *

A year or two into my research, I sat next to Mike Seaton in the lobby of First United Methodist Church while he told me that even though he lived forty-five minutes away, he commuted to First Church every week rather than attend a church closer to his home.[1] "I couldn't be a fundamentalist," he said, "I just couldn't. In my old church, I just couldn't believe what they said I had to believe. They were very into literal interpretations of the Bible, and if you said things there like you can say here, like 'I thought this' and 'I wondered about that' and 'I just can't believe that' and interpretations, people would come up to you afterwards and touch you on the shoulder and say 'I'll pray for you.' So I got to where I couldn't take it anymore, so I stopped going. And I didn't want to be totally secular, so I was foundering for a long time until this, the pastors here, this nonliteralism, brought me back. It was like a breath of fresh air. Things made sense that didn't make sense before, and I felt like I could be a Christian without giving up my *integrity*."

Mike has struggled with religion, and he's struggled with secularity, too. The kind of religion he was brought up in didn't sit right with him. It demanded that he twist his mind into a foreign shape, that he submit his own thinking to the creedal requirements of his church—that he believe the unbelievable. Trying to believe things that you don't actually believe is a constant psychological battle. But what if your community and the people you look to for leadership say you *must* believe these things, and believe them with all your heart? What if they tell you that being true to your religion means believing the right things, and that if you don't hold the right beliefs, then you're a lost soul? The challenge is compounded, and the choice seems clear: Be a religious person and be alienated from your own mind, or live with integrity and be alienated from religion.

Mike Seaton is not the only American to have felt confronted with this choice. In the course of my research, I heard many deep thinkers like Mike talk with pain and anger about what one called the "lock-step spirituality" of their childhood churches. Some felt, and still feel, a sense of deep betrayal, a sense of having been lied to by people they trusted during their most impressionable years. Some have never forgiven religion.

Another smaller but growing group of people were raised in families that weren't religious at all, or that were only nominally religious. These people were never confronted with a choice like Mike's, and some even have happy memories of candlelight Christmas Eves and Jesus loving the little children, all the little children of the world. Still, religion never seemed like much—it seemed mostly irrelevant and still, however softly, built around lists of beliefs that seemed both untenable and uninspiring. As they grew older, nonreligious and marginally religious people found it easy to drift away from religion or simply to reject it out of hand as an anti-intellectual institution.

Mike, though, didn't follow this path. He left his childhood church, but that didn't satisfy him. He was foundering for a long time, he said, because although he had left his old church, he "didn't want to be totally secular." Why not?

Voices bubble up from throughout the culture to answer this question. Two hundred miles from First United Methodist Church, Wayne Teasdale is giving a lecture at an adult education center called Common Ground. Wayne, an author, teacher, and monk, says, "Ancient people look at a river and ask, 'What does it mean?' Modern people have no idea it means anything; we've lost our capacity to ask." During a call-in radio program, author Winifred Gallagher says, "In a funny way it's actually our extreme secularism that's turning us back to spirituality . . . It's the sense of something missing in the midst of enormous material plenty that actually has people thinking about profound spiritual issues." Author Danah Zohar, in an interview, says, "We have a tremendous crisis of meaning as we go into this new century. The twentieth century was a kind of terrible spiritual vacuum during which our traditional religions lost their hold on us. . . . We've tried to take comfort in a lot of materialist grubbing, and just having lots of material goods, but in the middle of the night I think all of us lie there wondering what's it all about or why should I get up in the morning. Materialism is a kind of ineffective stop to our deep need for meaning."

People like Mike don't want to give up religion totally because the alternative is a secular culture that seems to be *missing* something—a sense of meaning, of larger purpose, of transcendent value. For many thousands of years, religion gave life its deepest meaning—it made life's events, tragedies, and joys significant in some larger, cosmic sense. Religion provided a sense of the transcendent, of truths that lie deeper than what our eyes can see and beyond what our rational minds can grasp. At its best, religion gives people a deep sense of orientation within the cosmos. For people like Mike, to lose religion is to succumb to a secular world that seems comparatively shallow, preoccupied with the least important, basest aspects of human life, and unable to see even the possibility of deeper meaning, more profound truths, or a richer experience of life.

These two alternatives—an unbelievable religion on one side, and a shallow, vacant secularity on the other—were equally unsatisfying to Mike. But what else was there? At first, and for a long time, he was foundering, disoriented. There didn't seem to be anything else; there didn't seem to be any third option.

This is the way the religious landscape looks to many Americans, especially to college-educated Americans like Mike: on one side, a dogmatic, arrogant, exclusive, and unbelievable religious traditionalism, and on the other, a spiritually vacant secular society obsessed with material gain and content to go through the motions of life without asking the deeper questions. Mike wanted something more.

What he found was First United Methodist Church, and an approach to religion that felt, as he told me, like a breath of fresh air. First Church's reflexive approach to spirituality not only allowed but actually encouraged Mike to raise questions about Christian tradition, and to define for himself which parts of the tradition held meaning for him and which parts he simply couldn't believe. At First Church, religious tradition and religious community did not represent hard-and-fast "answers" that he was to believe. Instead, they were resources he could draw on as he reflected on the big questions he had about life and meaning. For Mike, reflexive spirituality made religious tradition finally make sense.

*   *   *

Mike and I were coming from different places—he from a conservative Christian background, I from a mostly secular background with a smattering of mainline Protestantism left over from childhood. But we were both looking for meaning, and neither of us were finding it in the worlds we were coming from. We both found something of this meaning in reflexive spirituality.

This book was born of academic research and is grounded in sociological theory and systematic empirical observation. I hope that sociologists, and especially students, find it helpful. But as I wrote it, I was also thinking of educated seekers like Mike and me. A lot of people are wanting a sense of spiritual meaning in their lives. And a lot of people are frustrated in their search for meaning by forms of religiosity that seem to place limits on reason and by forms of secularity that lack spiritual depth. If you are one of these people, I hope that this book speaks to you personally. If, on the other hand, you are actively engaged in reflexive spirituality, then I hope that you find this book to be a useful mirror. I hope you recognize yourself in these pages, and I hope they help you as you continue to reflect on religion, spiritual meaning, and modern society.

1 REFLEXIVE SPIRITUALITY: FINDING MEANING IN MODERN SOCIETY

How can I find a spirituality that makes sense to me intellectually? How can I have an intellectual life that speaks to my soul? How can I find meaning in my life and in my religion?

These questions are central to the lives of educated spiritual seekers who find little meaning in either ordinary secularism or traditional religion. On one hand, secular life can seem spiritually empty, focused on the material, the practical, and the expedient, to the exclusion of deeper meanings. On the other hand, religious life can seem intellectually untenable, focused on lists of required beliefs, and dogmatic in a way that leaves no room for critical inquiry. Educated spiritual seekers are looking for something more than these two alternatives offer. They're looking for a spirituality they can sink their intellectual teeth into and a worldview that puts the mundane into meaningful perspective. Educated seekers are looking for the intersection between "what's inspiring" and "what makes sense."

Scholars who study religion in modern society ask a parallel set of questions: *What happens to religious tradition in a world that values critical thought? What's the relationship between modern reason and traditional faith? How do people find transcendent meaning in modern society?* These scholars know that religion holds a precarious place in modern society; that many aspects of modern life seem to chip away at religious meaning, that people sometimes use religion to voice opposition to patterns of modern life, and that the traditional and the modern often seem to be in overt conflict. What happens in such a state of tension? Scholars want to understand the nature of "religious modernity"—the way that the tensions between modern rationality and religious traditions play out.[1]

This book describes a kind of spirituality that speaks to both sets of questions: *reflexive spirituality* (a term coined by sociologist Wade Clark Roof). Reflexive spirituality is popular among educated seekers in a variety of religious traditions and also among people who think of themselves as spiritual but not religious.[2] *Reflexive* here has more to do with *reflection* than with *reflex*, and describes a habit of mentally "stepping back" from one's own perspective to reflect on it objectively. People who practice reflexive spirituality are committed to thoughtful reflection about their own spirituality in light of other possible spiritual perspectives. They are intentional, deliberate, and self-directed about their search for spiritual meaning. They do their best to take advantage of the huge variety of religious symbols and spiritual ideas that are available in the modern world. And they constantly search for new spiritual ideas, new sources of wisdom, and new images, stories, and rituals to consider incorporating into their own spiritual outlook.

The hallmark of reflexive spirituality—and what makes it so compelling for both educated seekers and scholars—is that it blasts apart ordinary conflicts between faith and reason in favor of searching for meaning wherever it can be found. People who practice reflexive spirituality seek to move beyond doctrine-centered religion but hold tightly to the idea of a transcendently meaningful universe. They spurn forms of rationalism that they see as narrow, but they use reason to find new meaning in religious symbols, stories, and traditions.

In reflexive spirituality, educated seekers are finding an answer to their desire for a spirituality that engages their intellect and an intellectual life that speaks to their soul. Educated seekers are looking for meaning: transcendent meaning, ultimate meaning, meaning-of-life kinds of meanings. To get this kind of meaning, they use the resources of both religion and reason. They apply intellectual tools to get more meaning out of the world's religious traditions, and at the same time, they draw on religious traditions to bring more meaning to ordinary secular life.

This book explores reflexive spirituality in depth. What is reflexive spirituality, and why does it matter? Where does it come from? What does it look like in practice? How do people use it to find religious meaning? Why are people embracing it? And what influence could it have on society more broadly?

I came to study reflexive spirituality because I wanted to understand how people were finding spiritual meaning in a society that values reason so strongly. Scholars have noticed tensions between reason and spiritual meaning, and they've developed theories about how these two things interact. But how do ordinary people deal with this tension? I wanted to know, so I went out and listened. I went to religious places like churches, secular places like public lectures and workshops, and "in between" places like interfaith education centers. In all these places, I listened for how people were talking about spiritual meaning and how they were relating spirituality to reason.

What I found was a spiritual culture that went beyond the boundaries of any particular religion and even of the religious sphere in general. This culture was like a language—a way of talking about religion and spirituality, transcendent meaning, and modern society. And people all over society were having a conversation in this language, both inside and outside religious institutions.[3] This book is an interpretation of that conversation—an explanation of the culture of reflexive spirituality in light of my driving theoretical questions about the relationship between transcendent meaning and modern rationality. The chapters that follow present reflexive spirituality as three things: a critique of modern culture, a way of relating to religious tradition, and a popular theology. Each of these aspects of reflexive spirituality is an effort to bring transcendent meaning into modern society.

Reflexive spirituality as a critique of modern culture. It can be hard to find meaning in modern life. Ordinary people know this from experience, and social theorists have identified specific reasons why this might be so, such as the growth of dehumanizing bureaucracies, the separation of life into different spheres built on competing values, and the declining power of religion.[4] Like these theorists, the reflexive spiritualists I observed identified a set of patterns in modernity—cultural priorities, habits of thought and perception—that they think makes it difficult to experience either life or religion as meaningful. They criticized these patterns and encouraged each other not to be bound by them. Modern society is too focused on the literal, they believed; too focused on the observable, measurable, and material; too focused on rules and routine at the expense of deeper purposes; and too eager for final answers and definitive conclusions to allow for mystery, complexity, and nuance.

As it happens, all these modern preoccupations are aspects of a particular kind of reason that scholars have sometimes called *technical reason* or *technological rationality*. Technical reason is about finding means to an end, and is excellent at helping us find the right methods to get as efficiently as possible to a given finish line. It's not so good, though, at helping us find meaning in life. Reflexive spiritualists think that we give too much power to technical reason, that it's become our default approach to life, and that we won't be able to experience life or religion as richly meaningful until we can think outside the technical box.[5]

Sociologists have sometimes observed religious groups criticizing modern society, and you only have to listen to Christian radio to hear regular criticisms of "the modern world," "modern culture," and "modernism" from conservative religious leaders. This kind of criticism—often focused on moral issues—is the kind that sociologists are most familiar with. It falls easily into a kind of "religion versus modernity" framework that sociology is heir to, because it seems in some ways to come from outside modernity and to represent a backlash from people who want to replace modern values with ones that they see as more Biblical, more Islamic, or generally more in line with their own particular religious tradition.

In reflexive spirituality, we see a different kind of religious criticism of modernity. It isn't conservative, it isn't focused on morality, it doesn't seek to establish the worldview of a particular religious tradition, and above all, it isn't hostile to modernity. It doesn't come from "outside," but from "inside" modernity; it isn't a backlash against modernity, but an attempt to improve modernity—to refine it from within. The philosopher Paul Ricoeur once said that he wanted "to go beyond criticism by means of criticism"; he meant that he wanted to use the tools of modern reason to expose the limits of modern reason.[6] And this is just what reflexive spiritualists are doing: they're standing inside the tradition of modern reason and pointing out ways that this tradition makes it hard for modern people to find spiritual meaning.

Reflexive spirituality as a way of relating to religious tradition. For thousands of years, religion has been the world's best source and record of spiritual meaning. Reflexive spiritualists want to get that meaning back. They want to mine the world's religions for meaning; they want to get as much meaning as possible out of religion. To do this, they use modern tools—tools of reason. Reflexive spiritualists promote metaphorical interpretation as a way of making religious scriptures, symbols, and practices as meaningful as possible. They promote a pluralistic attitude toward religion: they embrace all religions as potentially worthwhile sources of spiritual meaning. They value spiritual experience, practices that nurture spiritual experience, and theologies grounded in spiritual experience. And they promote reflexivity, an attitude of ongoing critical inquiry into religious meaning.

All these tools resonate with *intellectual reason*, which is different from technical reason. Intellectual reason helps us analyze, interpret, and synthesize ideas and information. It helps us dig deeper into texts and life events;

it's given us literary interpretation, linguistic analysis, and the discipline of comparative religious studies. Intellectual reason is all about making meaning, making sense, understanding, and investigating. Reflexive spiritualists use intellectual reason to make religion meaningful to modern ears.[7]

Sociologists have sometimes observed people making religion meaningful this way, especially since the 1960s. And metaphor, pluralism, spiritual experience, and reflexivity have sometimes made their way into sociological theories of what makes religion meaningful. Robert Bellah, for example, made the case for metaphor—what he called "symbolic consciousness"—in his 1970 book, *Beyond Belief.* He said that metaphorical interpretation makes it possible for us to find meaning in all the world's religions: "Symbolic consciousness is a way of outflanking literalism. . . . It thus frees us from being imprisoned in particular vocabularies at the same time that it makes all existing vocabularies available to us."[8] Andrew Greeley's theory of religion also emphasizes metaphor. In *Religion as Poetry*, he suggested that the heart of religion is the use of metaphor to express experiences of renewal.

Colin Campbell and William Swatos both observed people's growing interest in religious experience and pluralism; they saw this as a way that religions have adapted to the conditions of modern life. Robert Wuthnow has described an increasingly popular "spirituality of seeking" that "concentrates on that mixture of spiritual and rational . . . whereby the person in modern societies seeks meaning in life." Wuthnow says that the shift to a spirituality of seeking "consists of movement away from a denial of doubt (shielding people from questions about the existence of God) to a redefinition of doubt as the essence of reality (uncertainty as a fixture of the human condition)." In such a spirituality, "rather than rules, symbolic messages prevail." In a recent study of the culture of the American spirituality movement, Courtney Bender observed the importance of spiritual experience and the practices that support and give meaning to them; she said that these practices made "daily life . . . always possibly revelatory" and "any (or every) event . . . potentially meaningful."[9]

Jerome Baggett found reflexivity among American Catholics who were creating new religious meanings.[10] And of course, the term "reflexive spirituality" comes from Wade Clark Roof, who defined it as an ability to understand one's own spiritual view "as just that—*a view*" among other possible views. Roof described reflexive spirituality this way:

> It encourages a more open stance toward religious teachings and spiritual resources; more experiential and holistic views, and active incorporation of religious input into constellations of belief and practice, or greater agency on the part of an individual in defining and monitoring

one's own spiritual life. The effect is to create greater self-engagement with religious tradition . . . spiritual seeking is elevated as a prominent religious theme and can itself be a creative, revitalizing experience, even a venue to transforming the meaning of the religious itself.[11]

Together, these authors paint a picture of a spirituality engaged with metaphor, experience, pluralism, and reflexivity. But these are not just random features of contemporary spiritual culture: they go together as a package of tools that are perfectly suited to making life and religion meaningful for people who value intellectual reason. What's more, they're not simply a way that religions have adapted to modernity—they're also a religious attempt to influence the character of modernity—to make it more meaningful.

Reflexive spirituality as a theology. These tools lead reflexive spiritualists to a particular understanding of the divine, the sacred, or the transcendent. Reflexive spirituality isn't a religion, but a way of relating to religion, and it doesn't have a full-fledged, detailed theology. What it does have is a set of emphases: qualities of the divine that reflexive spiritualists find especially important. They see God as infinite, immanent—part of everything rather than a separate entity removed from ordinary life—and life-giving. Sociologists have sometimes made note of these kinds of theological themes in contemporary American spiritual culture. Robert Wuthnow, for example, said that spiritual seekers insist that "the sacred cannot be known fully." Courtney Bender noted that popular contemporary metaphysical writers have an immanent concept of the divine and don't want to "plac[e] a limit on the capacity of God." Wade Clark Roof observed that popular spiritual culture emphasizes a God that is both transcendent and immanent, "both 'right here' and 'beyond.'"[12]

These aren't new ways of thinking about God; they're longstanding features of a variety of theologies in several religious traditions. But these are the aspects of God that matter most to reflexive spiritualists, and there's a reason why: an infinite, immanent, vitalizing god is a god that makes ordinary life meaningful. It's a theology focused on meaning, on the possibility of meaning, on the possibility that there's more to life than meets the eye, and on the richness and profundity that that "more" can give to a life that might otherwise feel like going through the motions.

The Meaning of Meaning

What do we mean by "meaning"? When we say that people are looking for meaning, what is it that they're looking for? It's worth looking closely at this concept to understand the different kinds of meaning that make up our daily lives and the specific kind of meaning that most interests reflexive spiritualists.

At root, meaning is all about *connections* and *context*. A simple example is a traffic light. The color red by itself has no particular meaning, but in the context of a traffic light, it gains a very clear meaning because of its connections with yellow and green lights and traffic laws. For another ordinary example, I used to play a word association game with my introductory sociology students. I'd write a word on the chalkboard, and they'd respond by writing down the first word that came to mind. Then I'd gather their responses and tally them for all to see. One of the words I gave them was "party," and typically, out of twenty-six students, about sixteen of their responses referred to alcohol, about five referred to dancing, and the remainder referred to birthdays. Typically, no one responded with the names of political parties, and no one ever referenced other kinds of social groups or gatherings, such as wedding parties, housewarming parties, block parties, or Tupperware parties. For my students, the meaning of the word "party" had everything to do with their immediate context of college life. If I had asked a group of grade school students, a group of suburban adults, or a group of political operatives to tell me the first words that came to mind when I said "party," they would have come up with very different lists, because "party" would have a different *meaning* for each of them, based on each group's unique context and the connections they drew between "party" and other images.

Behaviors don't make sense—aren't meaningful—out of context. If, as I go through life, I'm bursting into song while dressed in a bell skirt and carrying a parasol, it doesn't make sense. If I'm on stage in a Civil War-era musical, it does. If I'm going door to door demanding chocolate from my neighbors, it doesn't make sense. If I'm a six-year-old dressed as Darth Vader and it's Halloween, it does. This connection between meaning and context is why people resent their comments being taken out of context—it's the context that makes their meaning clear.

We can go deeper with this idea of meaning, connections, and context. Many people, when asked what gives meaning to their lives, talk about their families. Connections between people give us meaning. A person becomes more meaningful to me if he marries my sister or is born to my best friend or hurts my mother or hires me. An argument is more meaningful to me if it takes place in the context of my family than it would be if I overheard it among a group of strangers. When people say they find meaning in nature, they're describing a connection they feel between themselves and the forest, the fields, the ocean, the sky. My hometown becomes meaningful to me by virtue of the many different connections I make between me and it—here is where I played in my first baseball game, here is where I used to go for walks, there is the landscape I used to see out my bedroom window. My city was my context, and so became meaningful to me.

When an idea is confusing, we try to make sense of it—make it meaningful—by connecting it with ideas we do understand, or by placing it in a larger context. Christians might try to understand the Buddhist idea of nirvana by considering it in connection to the idea of heaven. Movements for social justice make their concerns understandable by comparing them to other injustices. The women's movement, before articulating the idea of sexism, described a "sex-based caste system." The gay rights movement compares laws against gay marriage to laws prohibiting miscegenation, and connects anti-gay violence to lynching, placing both in a broader context of violence and domination. Comparing and contrasting, drawing connections, placing ideas in context—this is how we make new ideas meaningful.

When events are disturbing, we try to make sense of them—make them meaningful—by placing them in some larger context or by connecting them to other ideas. Recovering from a divorce or a serious illness often involves considering connections between our personal trauma and our past and future, our growth and development, our nature and character. Drawing these connections, placing our experience in the context of our lives, allows us to reorient ourselves, to respond meaningfully to experiences that throw so much into question.

Deep reflection often brings up more profound questions about existential meanings. How do I make sense of suffering, my own and that of others? How do I orient myself to death? How do I live my life in a way that is meaningful day by day? What is the nature of my connections to other human beings? How are people connected to nature and to other animals? How do I respond to profound beauty, extreme violence, and deep love? How do I orient myself to the sheer size and complexity of the universe? These questions ask for more profound meaning—Meaning of Life meaning—or what scholars call *transcendent* meaning. This kind of meaning, too, is about connections and context, but here we're talking about profound connections to an ultimate context. To *transcend* means to *go beyond*, and the *transcendent* refers to a context that goes beyond our ordinary lives and all our ordinary ways of understanding things, to give meaning to the whole.

How can we think about this idea of a transcendent context? Spatial images can help. I picture the earth surrounded by the universe, and imagine that metaphorically, the transcendent encompasses the mundane as the universe encompasses the earth. Or, consider your reaction to things that are really big—mountains, oceans, the night sky. I used to have an office right outside Pike's Peak. As I walked out of my office at the end of each day, I was often knotted up with daily preoccupations—this and that on my to-do list, the email I never responded to, the broken copy machine, assorted work-related dilemmas and relationship stresses—and then I would look at the mountain, which was one hundred thousand times older than me and 2,800 times taller than me, and feel that in some way it was that much bigger than my worries, as well. This is the feeling of the transcendent—the feeling of a much longer perspective, a much bigger order.

I also think about transcendent meaning from the point of view of a sociologist. Social scientists are in the business of making meanings. We make human experiences make sense by drawing connections and putting them in some kind of social, historical, political, or economic context. Social scientists can explain how racial inequality is perpetuated, how economies cycle through recession and growth, and how democracies become stronger and weaker. But all our explanations are necessarily partial and relative. What places society and history themselves in context? What does it mean that history happened that way and that society is organized this way? Social science can't address the whole of life, because it can't conceptualize a context for human experience that's larger than society and more enduring than history. That larger context is the transcendent.

Another way of thinking about transcendent meaning comes from the German sociologist Thomas Luckmann, who wrote about how transcendent meanings relate to more ordinary, everyday kinds of meaning. A helpful comparison here is to psychologist Abraham Maslow's theory of a *hierarchy of needs*, which suggests that people have fundamental needs and higher needs, and that people first seek to meet their fundamental needs and then move on to higher needs. Maslow's hierarchy is often pictured as a triangle divided into several layers, with physiological needs like food and water at the base, social needs like love and belonging in the middle, and more abstract needs like self-esteem and creativity at the top. Luckmann's theory of culture and meaning can be imagined in a similar way. In a short book called *The Invisible Religion*, Luckmann described culture as layered sets of meanings arranged in a nested hierarchy of significance, complexity, and abstraction.[13] At bottom, Maslow-like, are meanings we need to get along at the most fundamental level; for example, the simple categories we use to order the world around us: "trees, rocks, dogs, walking, running, eating, green, round, etc., etc."[14] A little higher up, we find higher levels of abstraction: "maize does not grow where aloe grows; pork is inferior meat; there should be no marriage between first-degree cousins; if invited for dinner take flowers to the lady of the house." Continuing our journey up the culture hierarchy, we pause at "early to bed and early to rise keeps a man healthy, wealthy and wise; a true warrior does not shrink from pain; and a lady does not smoke in public," climb up to "he lived and died a man," and arrive, near the top of our hierarchy of meanings, at "a just social order." At the very top of this pyramid are meanings that transcend everyday life—meanings that rely on symbols such as God, Nirvana, Tao, Brahman, Allah, Christ, and Unity Consciousness. Luckmann calls this layer of meanings "the sacred cosmos" and identifies it with the heart and substance of religion.

It is these meanings—transcendent meanings, spiritual meanings—that reflexive spiritualists are after. They want a larger context and deeper connections to help them find wisdom, insight, perspective—the meanings of life. They're interested in everything that might help them discover and create these meanings—including religion, reason, and anything else that offers wisdom.

The Research Behind *You Can't Put God in a Box*

This book's explanation of reflexive spirituality is based on several years of participant observation in settings where people had come together to talk, or to hear others talk, about transcendent meaning. Historically, transcendent meaning has been the institutional specialty of churches and other religious organizations. But these aren't the only places where people talk about spiritual meaning, so I didn't limit my observations to these kinds of settings. Instead, I studied places that fell along a spectrum from more religious to more secular. On the religious end, I studied a large United Methodist church, where I attended weekly services, Sunday School classes, and discussion groups. In the middle was Common Ground, an interfaith adult education center where I attended lectures and discussions on a variety of religious themes. On the secular end of the spectrum, I attended a variety of public lectures and workshops where people were talking about bringing a sense of meaning into their work and their lives; I also recorded and analyzed several talk radio and television programs in which participants were discussing spiritual meaning. All these settings were located near Madison, Wisconsin, and Chicago, where I was living when I was researching this book. In each setting, I took detailed notes on people's talk and then analyzed these field notes using coding and categorization methods developed by grounded theorists.[15] These three settings are the backdrop of this book.[16]

First United Methodist Church

First United Methodist Church is a large, urban church with a membership of a little over a thousand. I spent ten months attending weekly services and several discussion groups at First Church. The "Faith and Reason" group included about twenty-five people who met for an hour each month to talk about spirituality and the life of the mind. Two ongoing adult Sunday School classes, "Reading the Bible Intelligently" and "Theology for the Twenty-First Century," were led by a retired minister named Cecil Findley. I also attended one meeting of "Religions of the World," a class Cecil started after I had completed my field work. Cecil's classes, taught consecutively, drew between fifteen and forty people; some were "Cecil groupies" who attended whatever class he offered, some came just for particular classes, and a few attended just one or two meetings. Cecil's words appear often in the following pages. He was a friendly, gentle, intelligent man of about seventy who described himself as having been in a "lifelong lover's quarrel" with the Methodist Church on account of his liberal views.

Another church leader whose words appear often in this book is David Lyons, First Church's senior pastor for the first four months of my research there. David had served as senior pastor for twelve years before his retirement, and he began participating again as a member after twelve months of retirement. David would also have described many of his views as liberal, and he commented once that as he approached retirement, he had decided to reveal more of his personal opinions in his sermons than he had done in the past. David was a highly skilled preacher, an avid reader, and an outspoken man, and by all indications, he was never one to water down his sermons. His comment does suggest, though, that the sermons I excerpt in this book may be stronger statements of his honest opinions than he might have made earlier in his career. David's successor was a younger minister whose sermons were less theological—that is, they usually didn't focus on transcendent meaning but instead emphasized more everyday topics such as family relationships, church life, and emotions. As a result, David's successor does not appear in this book.

First Church was located near a large university, and it drew a number of well-educated community members. I didn't conduct a survey, but it's probably safe to say that most people who participated in the groups I studied had finished some college, and a few had advanced degrees. Churches are

America's most segregated social institution, and First Church was no exception: the membership was overwhelmingly white. Otherwise, the congregation seemed demographically unremarkable: the statistics I have suggest that besides a higher-than-average level of educational attainment, First Church's membership was fairly typical of large, urban, white, Protestant churches.[17]

Common Ground

Common Ground is a thirty-five-year-old adult education center located in one main branch and four smaller branches in and around Chicago. My research focused on Common Ground's original branch in Deerfield, a suburb about ten miles from the city limits. Common Ground's literature described the organization as "a study center whose primary focus is on the major religious, philosophical, spiritual, and cultural traditions and their implications." As an educational nonprofit organization, it sponsored year-round adult education classes that brought together different kinds of experts to give lectures and lead discussions several times a week. Many of these leaders were scholars in fields such as religious studies, philosophy, history, psychology, mythology, or astronomy; many were professional religious workers such as nuns, monks, or rabbis; some were artists or musicians.

Classes cost ten dollars each, typically lasted two hours, and were oriented around particular topics, such as "The Century's Top Five Religious Books," "Interdependence: The Heart of Buddhist Philosophy," "Biblical Portraits: The Matriarchs," "An Evening with Socrates," and "The Mystic Heart: Discovering a Universal Spirituality." Participants came to classes to learn about the wisdom of the world's traditions so that they could assimilate that wisdom into their own spiritual outlook.

Common Ground classes drew between ten and fifty people—most often, about thirty people attended. Classes took place in a classroom attached by a hallway to a church building, although Common Ground has never been affiliated with this or any church. Different people attended different events, two to three hundred people were regular participants at any given time, and at the time of my research (1997–2002), the organization's mailing list included five thousand people. The majority of participants were white and college educated. Their ages varied widely, but most were over forty. Their religious affiliations also varied widely, but most had some experience with Christianity and Judiasm. Most had learned a little (and some had learned a lot) about the other world religions, and a small number considered themselves Buddhists, Muslims, or members of other world religions. Typically, Common Grounders' identification with a particular religion was not exclusive—most considered all religious traditions to be valuable sources of meaning and wisdom. As an organization, Common Ground was not affiliated with any particular religion and considered itself to be actively interfaith. I attended Common Ground classes once or twice a week for six months. I also attended special events such as weekend retreats and discussions hosted in participants' homes.

Common Ground was the brainchild of two men whose voices appear frequently in this book. Ron Miller was a professor of religious studies at a small liberal arts college. He was about sixty years old and had attended a Jesuit seminary as a young man. During one class, he mentioned that he came up with the idea for Common Ground when he was a graduate student:

> What we were meeting with in these traditions was so exciting and, we felt, so important for the coming millennium. And yet we wanted to be in a space free of judgment, you're bad if you don't believe x. We wanted a *common ground* where we could come together as human beings, where you could look at the teaching and not have to deal with the rest of that "and of course *this* is the best, deepest, or most truthful."

Ron brought his idea to his friend Jim Kenney, a fellow graduate student, who later said, "Ron came to me and had this idea and I of course said, 'That's a stupid idea, it'll never work.'" Ron apparently wheedled his friend into helping him anyway, and the two of them codirected the organization. At the time of my research, Jim was close to being a full-time interfaith activist; he held instrumental positions in a variety of international interfaith organizations. A third Common Grounder whose words appear often in this book is Wayne Teasdale, one of the regular teachers, who was a Christian monk with a PhD in theology.

These three men were very active teachers during my time at Common Ground, and all three were extremely eloquent. I do quote other Common Ground participants throughout the book, but you'll see Ron, Jim, and Wayne most often.

Secular Cornucopia

The third set of field sites I studied was a collection of publicly advertised lectures, workshops, and media programs about meaning in modern life. I studied these settings to get a sense of reflexive spirituality as a diffuse cultural practice, spread throughout the culture, rather than one specific to particular kinds of organizations. Most of these events fall into two categories.

First, I studied talks and discussions associated with the Spirituality at Work movement. This movement is made up of a loose network of business people, scholars, and consultants who are working to bring spiritual responsibility and meaning into the world of commerce. These workers were frustrated with business practices that are only about the "bottom line," and they wanted businesses to integrate additional standards into their practices. The Association for Spirit at Work, for example, promoted "work as a spiritual path" and sought to "help create a critical mass in society that can help shift from a worldview that focuses primarily on materialism to one that incorporates social justice, spiritual values, concern for the environment, and a valuing of human development in our places of work."[18] Workers participate in the Spirituality at Work movement in various ways, from attending workshops and lectures to hiring spiritual coaches to help them make spiritually and ethically responsible business decisions. The Spirituality at Work events I attended were all affiliated with the Crossroads Center for Faith and Work, located in Chicago.[19] Typical participants at these events were middle-management-level workers in corporations, lawyers, bankers, or independent consultants in technological fields.

The second set of more secular settings I studied featured authors speaking about their recent books. I attended public lectures by Parker Palmer, Huston Smith, and Neale Donald Walsch; these lectures drew between one hundred and six hundred audience members. I also recorded a television program featuring Wayne Dyer and public radio call-in interview programs with Thomas Cahill, Vincent Crapanzano, Diana Eck, Winifred Gallagher, Elizabeth Lesser, Thomas Moore, Alan Lew, Huston Smith, A. N. Wilson, Dan Wakefield, and Danah Zohar.

I also attended an evening event called "Stardust, Telescopes, and God," sponsored by a Lutheran retreat center, which brought together an astronomer and a professor of religious studies to talk about the night sky with an audience of about twenty-five people.

How I Chose These Field Sites

There was a logic to my choices of Lakeside, Common Ground, and the secular events I studied. But at first, it wasn't obvious what kinds of field sites to investigate. If I had set out to study religion, it would have made sense to study churches, synagogues, and other religious organizations. If I had set out to study religiosity, it would have made sense to interview individuals about their religious beliefs and practices. But I set out to study how people who value reason find spiritual meaning. Where to go?

To figure this out, I again drew on theory. I began with the social-theoretical work of Thomas Luckmann, whose book *The Invisible Religion* explains that a lot of modern religion takes place outside of churches and the other institutions that we usually think of as religious. Anthropologist Victor Turner often wrote about the concept of liminality; his work suggests that people often do creative, interpretive work in spaces "in between" the routines and institutions of ordinary social life. Taken together, Luckmann's and Turner's work suggested to me that I look in the "in between" spaces, in spaces set aside for conversation about spiritual matters in general, rather than limiting myself to institutions that we usually think of as religious. So I began to find field sites by looking around for all possible kinds of settings where people might be talking about spiritual meaning in relation to rationality.[20]

To narrow these options down, I turned to cultural theory that emphasizes the importance of communication, language, and vocabularies. The authors of *Habits of the Heart*, for example, present culture as a set of languages— ways of talking about the things that matter to us. Other sociologists have further developed this idea of talk as central to culture. Reflexive spirituality is also a language—a language that people use to relate rationality to spiritual meaning.[21] So to identify field sites to study systematically, I followed the language. I listened for how people related spiritual meaning to rationality when they came together to talk about it. I borrowed from the theoretical sampling techniques of grounded theorists and chose field sites that provided "the greatest opportunity to gather the most relevant data about the phenomenon under investigation"—in this case, how people related spiritual meaning and reason.[22] I visited a variety of places where people were discussing spiritual themes, and settled on Common Ground as a setting where people talked about these ideas a lot.

My observations of Common Ground classes gave me some key categories of analysis to begin with. From there, I followed the spirit of grounded theorists' relational and variational sampling by looking for settings that were markedly different from Common Ground but that still spoke to the central concepts of spiritual meaning and reason.[23] I wanted to find a more religious setting, and because of the power that mainline Protestant churches have had in U.S. society, I looked for a mainline Protestant church where people were relating reason to spirituality. I found First United Methodist Church, where pastors and members engaged in many conversations about theology and the relationship between religion and reason. I also wanted to see how people talked about these ideas in more secular settings, and found the variety of sites that I described above. I was especially interested in the Spirit at Work movement because the corporate world has been dominated by the kinds of rationalities that social theorists have suggested are particularly threatening to meaning.

The Approach: A Method for my Madness

I have two aims with this book. First, the book describes reflexive spirituality as I observed it in these different settings and explains what reflexive spirituality is about and why it's important. Second, the book contributes to sociological understandings of the relationship between religion and modernity. I've concentrated on the first aim. I think of this book as putting a frame around a collection of patterns in American religious culture, giving those patterns a name (reflexive spirituality), and saying, "Look." Reflexive spirituality is interesting on its own—interesting in the way that it creatively combines reason and religion in the pursuit of meaning. But the second aim will speak particularly to scholars in the field, and for those scholars, I want to say a word about my methodology—the logic of this book's analysis and the relationship between my fieldwork and my theoretical agenda.

The research for *You Can't Put God in a Box* and the analysis of reflexive spirituality that I offer are grounded in the extended case method, a methodology that uses participant observation to enhance our theoretical understanding of society. When scholars use the extended case method, they look at specific cases in light of existing theory and use theoretically anomalous data to reconstruct the theory. Researchers seek out theory and cases that can speak to each other. Particular cases are seen not as generalizable exemplars, but instead as interpretive challenges for existing theory. The scholar uses particular cases to extend the relevant theory so that the theory can now apply to a wider range of empirical phenomena. To put it simply, the logic of the extended case method looks like this: We have theory on a particular topic, but that theory can't fully explain what I've observed in the particular case or cases that I'm looking at. So we can draw from these cases to add to that theory so that we now have a better theory.[24]

This book has begun with sociological theorizing about the relationship between modernity and religion and about the relationship between modernity and transcendent meaning. Sociologists have often written about the relationship between religion and modernity, but with a couple of exceptions, our questions about this relationship have usually asked about only one direction of this relationship. We've often asked how the advance of modernity has affected religion, but we've rarely asked how religion might affect the character of modernity. To put it in statistical terms, we've seen modernity as an independent variable—a kind of unmoved mover that grows and grows until it takes over everything—and religion as a dependent variable at the mercy of this juggernaut. So scholars have debated whether modernity weakens religion, strengthens it, or changes it, but they've always asked, "How is religion *affected by* modernity?"[25]

In reflexive spirituality, we see the opposite process: we see people using religion and reason together to critique modern social patterns in an effort to create a more meaningful modernity. In this sense, reflexive spirituality presents a challenge to our usual understandings of the relationship between religion and modernity: existing theory can't fully account for a kind of spirituality that seems to be part and parcel of a reflexive modernity, trying to affect the character of modernity from within. So the case of reflexive spirituality offers an opportunity to refine our theorizing about religion and modernity.

Meanwhile, a few social theorists and philosophers have directly addressed the problem of *meaning* in modern society. Max Weber, Anthony Giddens, and Jurgen Habermas have identified some of the ways that modern societies make finding meaning difficult. For Weber, intellectual rationality, or what he sometimes called scientific rationality, was modernity's primary threat to transcendent meaning. Giddens and Habermas attributed the modern loss of meaning to an overgrowth of formal rationality in a differentiated society; in other words, to the creation and dominance of large-scale political and economic systems and the instrumental, technological, routinized approach to life that they foster. But all three of these theorists agreed that intellectual rationality keeps religion from making modern life meaningful.[26]

In reflexive spirituality, we see people creatively combining intellectual rationality and religious tradition in an attempt to make modern society more meaningful. People who practice reflexive spirituality want to take the best from modernity—its scholarship, its commitment to reason and evidence-based argument, and its unprejudiced embrace of knowledge wherever it can be found—and combine it with the best of religion—its wisdom, its symbolic potency, and its respect for knowledge that transcends reason—to bring a vibrant sense of transcendent meaning to modern society. Reflexive spirituality challenges existing theory by suggesting that intellectual rationality can help religion provide meaning to modern people.

Finally, the hermeneutical philosopher Paul Ricoeur also directly addressed questions of meaning in modern society. Like Habermas and Giddens, Ricoeur identified modern society's greatest obstacle to meaning as an overgrowth of formal rationality, and especially of the technological approach to life that these formal systems foster. But Ricoeur thought that intellectual rationality could revitalize religion so that religion could once again be a source of transcendent meaning in modern society. Riceour's ideas have informed my thinking about reflexive spirituality. But Ricoeur was a philosopher, not a sociologist, and his work doesn't tell us how the relationship between intellectual reason and spiritual meaning might play out in real life. Grounded as it is in systematic observation of people talking about these things in real life, the case of reflexive spirituality gives empirical dimension to Ricoeur's philosophy.[27]

2 REFLEXIVE SPIRITUALITY IN CONTEXT

Reflexive spirituality is like a character in a set of stories about changes in social and religious life that have taken place over the past three hundred years. This chapter tells four stories that help explain where reflexive spirituality comes from and why it matters:

1. The story of how modern society lost a sense of meaning
2. The story of how the discipline of sociology came to define religion as unmodern
3. The story of how progressive religion lost and rediscovered the language of myth
4. The story of the contemporary spiritual-but-not-religious movement and its changing relationship to religious tradition.

The themes of these four stories are the themes that define reflexive spirituality: reason, religion, and meaning. In each story, reflexive spirituality brings these themes together, as reason and religion both become resources in the search for spiritual meaning.

Story One: Disenchantment and the Modern Loss of Meaning

Images of a vague sense of meaninglessness or lifelessness abound in popular culture and the arts—consider T.S. Eliot's poem "The Waste Land" or the comic strip "Dilbert." These themes are especially popular at the movies. In 1967's *The Graduate*, for example, Dustin Hoffman's character Benjamin Braddock succeeds beautifully on the expected proving ground for academically talented young men: an elite East Coast college. Ben has been an athletic star and an extracurricular leader, and after graduating with honors, he arrives home in a daze, never asking aloud the questions that underlie his ennui: Is this all there is? What now? The most he can say is that he wants his future to be "different." We see his alienation more than we hear it, in his wide eyes, stony expression, and reluctance to be with other people. We see it too in his behavior at a graduation party hosted by his wealthy suburban parents for their wealthy suburban friends. Amid everyone's smiles, congratulations, and questions about his future, Ben dangles purposelessly in underwater silence in the corner of his parents' swimming pool, encased in the Darth Vader-like wetsuit his parents had given him as a graduation present and insisted he show off for everyone. Then his father's friend takes him aside and famously says, "I just want to say one word to you—just one word. Are you listening? Plastics."—whereupon Ben runs upstairs to hide in his bedroom.

In 1989's *Say Anything*, John Cusack's character Lloyd Dobler graduates from high school with fewer honors and fewer prospects than his valedictorian girlfriend, Diane Court. Diane's father, suspicious that Lloyd isn't good enough for his fellowship-winning daughter, asks Lloyd about his plans for the future, and Lloyd replies, "I don't want to sell anything, buy anything, or process anything as a career. I don't want to sell anything bought or processed, buy anything sold or processed, or process anything sold, bought, or processed, or repair anything sold, bought, or processed—you know—as a career. I don't want to do that."

In the 1999 film *Fight Club*, Edward Norton's character is a nameless automobile company employee whose job is to travel to accident sites to determine whether the company should issue product recalls, basing his decisions not on risks to human life, but on cost–benefit analyses of likely lawsuit settlements versus cost of recall. He describes his alienation: "You wake up at Seatac, SFO, LAX. You wake up at O'Hare, Dallas-Fort Worth, BWI. Pacific, mountain, central. Lose an hour, gain an hour. This is your life, and it's ending one minute at a time." When the movie opens, the character is trying to fill the emptiness in his life by filling his apartment to resemble the IKEA catalogue he peruses while sitting on the toilet, asking himself, "What kind of dining set defines me as a person?" Tyler Durden, the narrator's alter-ego, says, "Our generation has had no Great Depression, no Great War. Our war is spiritual. Our depression is our lives."

The contemporary comedy classic about modern alienation is 1999's *Office Space.* Peter Gibbons's life is the picture of suburban standardization: he works in an office park at a software company called Initech inside one of a hundred identical gray cubicles backed by a banner reminding employees that with every decision they make, they should ask themselves, "Is it good for the *Company?*" Peter has eight bosses, each of whom approaches him separately to reprimand him about a missed cover sheet on one of his reports and promises to send him another copy of the memo describing the new cover-sheet procedure. Peter's coworkers and bosses are caught in a bureaucratic maze of malfunctioning office equipment, fights over staplers, impersonal rules about the appropriate volume and hours for listening to the radio, and the scripted friendliness of customer service. ("Corporate Accounts Payable, Nina speaking—just a moment," chirps the receptionist at the cubicle across from Peter's several times a minute all day.) This spirit-numbing routine is broken up only by lackluster birthday parties, Hawaiian shirt day, and coffee breaks at Chotchkie's, a "family fun" restaurant that serves Pizza Shooters, Shrimp Poppers, and Extreme Fajitas and requires its waitstaff to "express themselves" via company-provided pins called "flair." The plot of the movie is driven by Peter's alienation from his job, and consequently his life, which he describes to his therapist this way: "So I was sitting in my cubicle today, and I realized, ever since I started working, every single day of my life has been worse than the day before it. So that means that every single day that you see me, that's on the worst day of my life."

Thoreau said the mass of men lead lives of quiet desperation, and a century later, the author of *The Tao of Pooh* said, "The desperation may have been quiet *then*, we suppose. *Now*, it's deafening."[1]

Sociologists call this state of affairs *disenchantment*. A disenchanted world is a flat, gray world, a world without enthusiasm, color, creativity, or spark. A disenchanted world is spiritually vacant, lacking in mystery, and strangely mechanistic. In a disenchanted world, people experience life as cogs in a machine, losing touch with their deeper humanity and relating to other people as though they are tools to be used rather than human beings to be truly known. Disenchantment was an important idea for the classical German sociologist Max Weber, who in a 1919 speech told his audience, "The fate of our times is characterized by rationalization and intellectualization and, above all, by the 'disenchantment of the world.' Precisely the ultimate and most sublime values have retreated from public life."[2] As his reference to values suggests, Weber thought of disenchantment as a loss of *meaning* in life. And as his references to "our times" and "public life" suggest, Weber thought of this loss of meaning not as a problem faced only by particular individuals in moments of crisis, but rather as a problem of the social system itself, and consequently a problem uniquely characteristic of modern life.

What caused modern society to become disenchanted? For Weber and like-minded sociologists, the story of disenchantment is driven by a historical process called *rationalization*. When a society is rationalizing—a process that unfolds over decades and centuries—it is gradually reshaping itself according to standards of *systematic reason*. Reason—rather than tradition—becomes the main standard a society uses to organize its social institutions, to evaluate ideas, and to decide on courses of action. The sociological story of rationalization and disenchantment goes like this.[3]

At one time, Western society was organized in a much simpler way. Instead of having separate institutions for the family, education, the economy, government, and religion, all of these systems were integrated. The family, for example, educated children, determined social status, arranged marriages to make economic and political alliances, acted as the center of economic production, and provided political leadership in the form of family elders who laid down the law. Ancestors were connected to gods or were gods themselves, and these ancestor-gods set in place the society's entire way of life. Religion was not a separate social institution; instead, it was what sociologist Peter Berger has called a "sacred canopy" that brought the whole of society together under one unifying set of ideas, stories, and traditions.[4] This sacred canopy infused life with meaning by giving every aspect of life a spiritual underpinning. To use Weber's terms, the sacred canopy of religion made earlier societies enchanted places to live.

Then, in the eighteenth century, the European Enlightenment changed everything. Systematic reason became the new standard for truth, morality, and social order, and from that point on, Western society has become more and more rationalized. In part, this process of rationalization meant separating out the different spheres of life so that each could operate according to its own logic and pursue its designated goals. Now we have The Economy for the pursuit of wealth, Education for training children, Politics for negotiating group interests, and The Family for love and caretaking. Religion, which once provided a sacred canopy of meaning that integrated all of life, is now just another social institution that people step into for moral education and emotional support, and step back out of for daily life. Individuals might continue to find personal meaning in religion, but this meaning is no longer reinforced outside the religious sphere. No longer are society's political process, system of economic distribution, and cultural narratives grounded in a respected religious tradition. Instead, each follows its own logic of competition, supply and demand, or commercial appeal and promotes its own ultimate values of economic growth, acquisition of power, or profit.

When religion becomes separated from the rest of life like this, people start to see it as an otherworldly fantasyland, irrelevant to the concerns of ordinary daily life. At best, it seems like a haven for ideals that are nice, but naïve. I might go to church and hear about brotherly love, but what do I do with that when I have to choose between laying off masses of employees and letting my company lose profits? I might learn from my religion about compassion and forgiveness, but what do I do with that when my country goes to war? My religion might encourage me to place spiritual values ahead of material values, but my boss tells me to maximize profits, and my president tells me to go shopping to stimulate the economy. Religion is disjoined from daily life, and weakened. It is no longer able to provide compelling meanings that tie everything together, that give daily life a sense of purpose, that help people experience themselves as transcendently connected to all that is, all that came before, and all that will be. The world seems to operate as a spiritless machine, and people feel like they're on a treadmill, running just to stand still, going through the motions for uncertain reward rather than living a life infused with significance and purpose. By separating religion from the other spheres of life, rationalization sucks the spirit out of daily life.

Rationalization also drains the meaning out of religion, and consequently out of society, in a second way, one more in line with our ordinary sense of what "reason" means. This kind of rationality has to do with the mind, with truth, with habits of thought and perception, and with ideas about the nature of reality. Max Weber called it *intellectual rationality*, or intellectualization.[5] Intellectual rationality is systematic reason applied to the world of ideas, and it is the heart of reflexivity. It's what colleges and universities call "critical thinking," and it demands that we ground our conclusions on logical inquiry and systematically collected evidence. A society built on intellectual rationality habitually practices systematic doubt, insisting, as sociologist Anthony Giddens has said, that "all knowledge takes the form of hypotheses: claims which may very well be true, but which are in principle always open to revision and may at some point have to be abandoned."[6]

How did the advent of intellectual rationality affect religion? First, it inflated the importance of *doctrine*: in an intellectually rational society, what matters is not what you do, or how you feel, but what you *believe*. So religion became all about belief in the accuracy of particular "facts"—but these facts came into conflict with the more convincing facts offered by that pinnacle of intellectual rationality, science.[7] The result is the familiar story of conflict between religion and science, faith and reason, expressed in public debates over heliocentrism, evolution, and the age of the earth. Intellectual rationality also undermined religion by undermining the idea of a totally authoritative, all-encompassing tradition in the first place. In a reflexive modernity, reason, not tradition, is the arbiter of truth, and no sacred canopy can stay aloft with critical thought constantly shooting darts at it.

Rationality, then, renders religion not only irrelevant, but also unbelievable. A reflexive society promotes skepticism toward anything that smacks of "irrationality"—such as religious faith, spiritual experience, or belief in a transcendent reality. If you can't see it, touch it, taste it, smell it, or hear it, it isn't real. Intellectual rationality drains meaning from religion by rendering the whole thing absurd. Invisible spirits? Mystical oneness with the universe? Life after death? "Come on," intellectual rationality says, "how could you seriously believe any of that? Where's the evidence?"

This is the sociological story of the disenchantment of the world. For millennia, it was religion that made life meaningful. But in modern times, a rationality with imperialistic tendencies has made religion seem irrelevant, naïve, unintellectual, and vaguely crazy. The result is a disenchanted world—a world without spirit, zest, depth, or meaning. In this story, reflexive spirituality appears as a surprise, and almost as a contradiction in terms. If reflexivity undermines religious faith, then what would it mean to relate to religion with this same rational-critical thought, this same practice of systematic doubt?

Spiritualities of all kinds have seen an upsurge in popularity lately, both inside and outside of religion.[8] In the context of this story of disenchantment, all the spiritualities we see emerging these days can be seen as efforts to re-enchant modernity. What's special about reflexive spirituality is exactly this engagement with reason, exactly this relationship to our reflexive modernity. Religion and reason have met before, but reflexive spirituality engages both reflexively. Reflexive spiritualists value both religious tradition and systematic reason but relate critically—reflexively—to both. Neither gets a pass. Neither has its assumptions taken for granted. Instead, each is mined for what it can contribute to the project of making modern life meaningful—the project of re-enchanting the world.

Story Two: Sociology, Religion, and the Project of Modernity

The discipline of sociology was born from crisis. The eighteenth and nine-teenth centuries in Europe were marked by massive social change. Centuries of monarchy were being replaced by the beginnings of modern democracy. Feudalism transitioned into capitalism. The Industrial Revolution marked a shift from economies based on manual labor to the beginning of the machine age and the emergence of large-scale factory production. These economic shifts led to rapid urbanization as displaced farm workers moved to the cities in search of manufacturing work. The scientific revolution had begun, bring-ing with it the new emphasis on reason and critical thought described in the last section.

From the perspective of the twenty-first century, we can look back and describe these changes as a transition from one kind of society to another. For people living through it, though, it was chaos. The social system that had been in place for centuries was coming apart, and no one really knew what would replace it or indeed if anything would replace it. Which of the new social ex-periments would last? What would they be like? Would democracy work? Would capitalism last, or would it self-destruct? What kinds of people, what kinds of relationships, would survive the anonymity and confusion of the overcrowded and dirty metropolis?

The discipline of sociology emerged as scholars who had originally been trained in economics, philosophy, history, and law tried to come to terms in-tellectually with the changes around them and influence the direction these changes would take. These early sociologists saw an underlying theme in the chaos. Tradition, the principal social power for much of human history, was losing its hold. In place of tradition was a new emphasis on individual initia-tive. People were taking things into their own hands by taking advantage of their capacity for rational thought. The mood of the times was one of progress and liberation from the shackles of tradition: no longer will society be run by kings, priests, and a powerful aristocracy whose authority depended on he-redity and divine right. Now, society will be run by the people themselves—through enterprise, free inquiry, free elections, and above all else, through the use of their God-given capacity for reason.

The storyline, then, was Oppressive Tradition Gives Way to Liberating Reason. To be modern was to reject tradition, and that meant rejecting the sacred canopy of religion that had held all the old traditions together. It was religion that gave monarchs divine right, that explained the nature of life and the movements of the universe, and that prescribed moral rules and social roles. In every way, religion seemed to be the hallmark and the guardian of the traditional social order. Religion, like tradition in general, had kept people shackled and constrained, tied to old ways of doing things and old ways of thinking. If modernity was a move away from tradition, then it must also be a move away from religion.

In essence, the discipline of sociology *defined* religion out of the modern picture. Sure, religion may still be strong in some populations, but then those populations are either antimodern or else distanced from the urban centers of modernity and the accoutrements of modern life in general. The more modern, the less religious. The disciplinary term for this idea is the theory of *secularization*, which proposes that as societies modernize, religion loses social power. Secularization theory emphasizes social power: it recognizes that religion may continue to offer comfort to individuals as a kind of "haven in a heartless world," but holds that at a broader level, religion comes to lose influence over the conditions of modern life. This was the dominant line of thought, particularly in European sociology, throughout most of the twentieth century. In recent years, as conservative religion has become such a noticeable social presence, sociologists have debated, amended, and sometimes outright rejected the theory of secularization. Many sociologists, however, interpret the rise of conservative religion within the either-or framework of secularization theory, describing it as a backlash against the conditions of modernity by groups who have been harmed by modernity's effects.[9]

The rise of conservative religion has gotten a lot of airplay on the nightly news, and as a consequence, many Americans have come to see religion as an inherently conservative phenomenon.[10] But conservative religion is only one part of the recent resurgence in religious life. Reflexive spirituality represents another kind of religious renaissance, one taking place among liberal religious groups, outside mainstream religion, and sometimes even within conservative religion. Because reflexive spirituality is grounded on both modern rationality and religious tradition, it doesn't fit the easy formulas of modernity versus tradition and reason versus religion. On the contrary, it is the deliberate, conscious, creative interaction of reason and tradition that produces reflexive spirituality's vitality and strength.

Reflexive spirituality, as a religious movement that prioritizes both reason and tradition, brings up the possibility of more complex relationships between these phenomena than sociologists have been used to considering. Seen through the lens of reflexive spirituality, modernity is not so much a movement away from religion, or even a movement away from tradition, but rather a movement toward a different way for people to relate to tradition.

Reflexive spirituality makes it clear that modernity is not inherently antagonistic to religion at all. Reflexive spirituality shows us how intellectual reason can actually enhance and strengthen religion, and points to the possibility that religious tradition might itself contribute positively to what social theorist Jurgen Habermas has called "the unfinished project of modernity."[11]

Reflexive spirituality suggests that Almighty Reason has become constraining in some ways, and yet remains liberating in other ways. People who practice reflexive spirituality use reason to strengthen religion at the same time as they use religion to critique and heal aspects of modernity that limit the possibilities for meaning. When we look at reflexive spirituality, we see a dynamic relationship between religion and modernity—a relationship of mutual influence in which neither one's assumptions are taken for granted and each is used to strengthen the other. If we want modernity to be an age of liberation, maybe religion can play a creative role in pushing this liberation further—this time, liberating us from some of the limitations of modernity itself.[12]

Story Three: Progressive Religion's "Third Way"

One of the challenges modernity brought to religion was a different way of thinking about authority and truth. Medieval Christianity had built its sense of truth on the twin foundations of Christian myth and its interpretation by ecclesiastical authority. When the modern cult of reason hit in the eighteenth century, it presented new foundations for truth: observable fact and its interpretation by individuals using their natural capacity for reason. How did Christianity respond?

On the question of ecclesiastical versus individual authority, the church effectively split down the middle. What we now call conservative Christianity placed its highest faith in external authority: the truth is Out There, in the authority of the church and in the Bible as church authorities interpreted it. It became the job of the church to resist the secularizing and infidel influences of modern culture. What we now call liberal Christianity, even as it maintained a church structure and defined itself through the Bible and the person of Jesus Christ, came to place ultimate faith in internal authority: the truth is In Here, in individual experience and reason. It became the church's job to reinterpret and rearticulate Christian truth in ways that made sense to modern ears.

On the question of myth versus fact, the split was more complex. Both liberal and conservative Christianity accepted the redefinition of "truth" to equal "fact." For conservative theologians, this meant redefining Christian scriptures as a set of facts instead of a set of myths, and holding to their accuracy in the face of challenges from modern science and history. For liberal theologians, this meant a two-hundred-year process of reevaluating and reimagining the Christian story in response to both scientific findings and the realities of life in modern society.

This two-hundred-year process is the story told by theologian Gary Dorrien in several comprehensive and definitive histories and analyses of liberal American theology; since theology is not my area of expertise, I have relied heavily on Dorrien's work for my knowledge in this area.[13] For Dorrien,

> Liberal theology is defined by its openness to the verdicts of modern intellectual inquiry, especially historical criticism and the natural sciences; its commitment to the authority of individual reason and experience; its conception of Christianity as an ethical way of life; its favoring of moral concepts of atonement; and its commitment to make Christianity credible and socially relevant to contemporary people.[14]

Over the years, liberal Christian theology developed additional themes that mark it as one of the parents of reflexive spirituality:

- Increasing openness to multiple religions, including first the Protestant denominations, then Christianity more broadly, then non-Christian religions
- Interest in the richness of metaphor and rejection of literal interpretation of scriptures
- Abstract and immanent images of God: God as a dimension of everything that is; God surrounding us; God as the spirit of love
- Ongoing creative renewal, fueled by a willingness to self-criticize and to engage criticism from outside.

From its earliest beginnings, liberal Christianity has defined itself as a "third way" between conservative Christianity and atheistic secularism. Except for a brief period of dominance in the early 1900s, this "third way" has always been under the radar. Conservative Christianity, in defining itself against modernism, ensured itself both headlines and a clear identity. Liberal Christianity wanted to engage the modern world on its own terms, and to the extent that it succeeded, it also lost, in that it became unremarkable.

In trying to speak to modern ears, liberal Christianity found itself in a difficult relationship with its own mythology. Enthralled by reason and science, and convinced by fact rather than idea, nineteenth- and twentieth-century people were increasingly skeptical of miracles, mysticism, and the transcendent in any of its forms. These were the prejudices of a rationalistic society: soon it wasn't *science* that was the standard for truth, but *scientism*—the belief that only that which can be established using the methods of science can be true.[15] Dorrien points out that even though liberal theology values internal authority, it made an external authority out of modern culture. It succeeded in speaking to modern ears by dampening the language of transcendence, by translating its miracle stories into morality fables, and by focusing on social justice and personal goodness rather than divine salvation.

Scholars sometimes call this liberal Christianity's "compromise" with modernity, and the implication is that liberal Christianity ultimately weakened itself by throwing out its baby of spiritual transcendence with the bathwater of religious language that no longer worked for people.[16] Ultimately, many people came to see liberal churches as places to go for moral education and social participation and not much else. Church attendance dropped as new generations of congregants found other avenues for their social justice or community activism pursuits and said to themselves, "I don't need to go to church to learn how to be a good person." This pattern of attrition and cultural blending has continued to the point that many liberal Christians are now cautious about describing themselves as Christian, recognizing that in the broader culture, "Christian" has come to mean "religious conservative."

But that's not the end of the story. The last decades of the twentieth century saw what Dorrien calls a "hidden renaissance" in liberal theology.[17] One main feature of this renaissance was the rediscovery of myth. As rationalism failed to satisfy human needs, and as conservative religions began to flourish in response, liberal theologians began to recover the language of transcendence, spirituality, the sacred, and mythical imagination. Theologians and other scholars began to think of myth as a valuable mode of understanding, different from history and different from fable. Myths are ideal for communicating spiritual insight and wisdom, transcendent meaning, sacred truths, and ultimate values. The language of myth is uniquely capable of evoking the ground of being, the depth dimension of life, and the ineffable—that which can't be communicated with the flat language of literalism. Scholars who are interested in myth think that it's essential to distinguish myth from fact, but that it's also essential to retain the language and spirit of myth. For a long while, "myth" has been synonymous with "lie" in the modern mind. In today's liberal theology, myths symbolize deep truths that are eviscerated when forced into literalistic interpretations.[18]

In later chapters, you'll read about Cecil, a retired Methodist minister who espoused this metaphorical, myth-centered approach to the Bible. In discussing these themes during an adult Sunday School class one day, Cecil told a story about his seminary days back in the 1950s. "I was so excited about these ideas; I found them so liberating, and I went up to my professor after class and said, 'This is wonderful! But how do I tell this to the people in my church?' And the professor said, 'Good heavens! Don't tell the people!'"

Reflexive spirituality is not a wholly new way of relating to religion. Many of its themes have been standard curriculum in seminaries for over fifty years. In reflexive spirituality, these themes have spread to "the people." In some ways, reflexive spirituality represents a democratization of the spirit of liberal Protestant theology. Now, "the people" are discussing and debating the relationships between myth and truth, science and transcendence, and individuals and scriptures. Discussions are bubbling up in liberal churches across the country, forming a grassroots religious movement interested in rebuilding a robust popular liberal Christian theology. An umbrella organization has emerged and grown along with the movement: The Center for Progressive Christianity defines itself with eight points, two of which are "We recognize the faithfulness of other people who have other names for the way to God's realm, and acknowledge that their ways are true for them, as our ways are true for us," and "We find more grace in the search for understanding than we do in dogmatic certainty—more value in questioning than in absolutes."

So is reflexive spirituality, at heart, just the latest incarnation of liberal Protestantism? No. It intersects with liberal Protestantism, and thrives on the connection. But we see reflexive spirituality not only in other religions, but also outside of religion altogether. The Jewish Reconstructionist Federation, for example, says that Jewish Reconstructionists are "challenged to enter the conversation of the generations and to hear voices other than our own, but to add our own voices as well," that "tradition has a vote, but not a veto," and that they "retain the traditional language of Jewish prayer, but not the obvious understanding of its meaning and function."[19] Aleph, the Alliance for Jewish Renewal, says that its members "worship in ways that honor both our tradition and intuition" and that they find wisdom and insight in Jewish sacred texts and traditions but that they also

find elements in what we have inherited that are historically limited and in need of re-interpretation or transcending. We . . . wrestle with their content and meaning, and decide what to draw on and what to leave behind. . . . We also draw on the wisdom of modern and critical scholarship, which adds insight and new perspectives to our study of philosophy and history.

Aleph also embraces religious pluralism:

We recognize with joy that Judaism participates in a world-wide exploration of the spiritual and commit ourselves to be in conversation with other spiritual paths, sharing what we discover and incorporating what we learn. . . . We pledge to continue developing and practicing that which is especially Jewish while knowing that it is in the sharing that we all are fulfilled.[20]

Meanwhile, plenty of Americans now describe themselves as "spiritual, but not religious"; they are participating in a spiritual life that isn't housed in a particular religious institution or focused on a particular tradition. In the broadest, most "secular" strands of reflexive spirituality, the attitude is really "wisdom and meaning wherever I can find it." Jesus, the Buddha, Lao-tzu, the Dalai Lama, poets, novelists, Oprah Winfrey, therapists, life coaches, movies, and any number of sources of insight are all valued together.[21]

So reflexive spirituality isn't just about liberal Christianity, or even liberal religion. But when it is practiced within a specific religion, reflexive spirituality focuses on that tradition—on reinventing, reinterpreting, and rearticulating scriptural stories, religious rituals, and theological principles. In churches, synagogues, and temples, reflexive spirituality acts as a revitalization movement among religious liberals.

Story Four: The Secret Tradition of the Spiritual-But-Not-Religious

Spirituality is about depth and vitality. People who want a rich spiritual life are looking for a deeper awareness, a heightened consciousness; they want to experience more of the meaning and intricacy of life. They want to feel truly alive—to feel engaged, to find life compelling. They want to feel centered and grounded in something eternal. They want a sense that there's more there than meets the eye. They want a little bit of magic. They want an antidote to what they experience as the flat, literalistic materialism of modern society— an antidote to its shallowness and apparent meaninglessness. They want a broader base, a deeper foundation, and a higher horizon.

Churches have responded to the resurgence of interest in spirituality by offering ways for people to cultivate a sense of connection to God, to each other, and to their own spiritual nature: one-on-one spiritual direction, Taizé services centered on group singing and meditation, meditative labyrinths, passionate devotional praise music, creative arts programs, and small groups for people to discuss spiritual books or their own spiritual development. But the spirituality movement isn't limited to what happens inside churches. In fact, the resurgence of spirituality in churches often goes unnoticed in light of the spectacular spiritual creativity that's been going on outside religious institutions over the past few decades. The larger spirituality movement offers meditation retreats, journaling instruction, Sufi-inspired dance rituals, Native American–inspired drum circles, life coaches encouraging people to get in touch with their inner guidance or higher self, women's magazine articles on finding the spiritual in everyday life, unique organizations such as the Omega Institute and the Institute of Noetic Sciences, and the Dalai Lama on television talk shows. And books, books, books: in decades past, bookstores had sections labeled "religion" that featured Bibles and academic theology. Now, bookstores have separate sections for each of the world's religions, plus comparative religion, spirituality, metaphysical, and personal growth sections, which together offer books about the soul, creativity, Jewish history, the historical Jesus, the Dalai Lama, Toltec wisdom, mythology, techniques for living in the present, histories of God, methods for finding a purpose in life, the insights of the dying, near-death experiences, the neuropsychology of religious experience, angels, individual spiritual memoirs, and many other topics.

My parents, born around 1940, just before the postwar Baby Boom, grew up thinking of spirituality as the same thing as religion, or as an aspect of it. You found spirituality in your religion. My students, born in the 1980s and 1990s as the children of the Baby Boomers, take for granted that spirituality and religion are different. It is the Baby Boomers who brought about this definitional shift, as they brought about a larger cultural shift that promoted humanistic values, personal growth, and individual autonomy. The generation of Watergate and Vietnam distrusted society's institutions: they saw them as constraints on individual freedom and opportunities for dangerous centralization of power. Religious institutions, it seemed to them, squelch the creative individual by encouraging unquestioning submission to external authority. Spirituality, by contrast, was about personal development, and required inner growth and access to inner resources. In the Boomer/counterculture analysis, religion hindered spiritual growth. Now, "spiritual but not religious" is a category on match.com. An Internet dater, asked "What is your faith?" can check boxes for Agnostic, Atheist, Buddhist/Taoist, four varieties of Christian, Hindu, Jewish, Muslim, Spiritual but not religious, Other, or No Answer.[22]

Because of all the creative ferment going on in relation to spirituality, and because of the creative energy the Boomers brought to propagating noninstitutional spirituality, it can seem as though the spirituality movement is new. People of all generations become more interested in religious matters as they grow into their forties and fifties, and the spirituality movement brings Boomer interests in humanistic values, personal growth, and individual autonomy to the sphere of religion. In reality, though, the contemporary American spirituality movement has its own history, and is drawing on a specific spiritual tradition that predates the Baby Boomers. This tradition has long roots in colonial occult practices, Platonic metaphysics, German Idealism, British Romanticism, Swedish mysticism, and liberal Protestantism, but it really began to come together as a coherent, identifiable spiritual tradition with the Transcendentalists in the 1830s.[23]

The Transcendental Club was led by Ralph Waldo Emerson and included several Unitarian ministers and former Unitarian ministers, all educated at Harvard Divinity School, as well as several teachers and writers interested in progressive thought. The Transcendentalists found the divine within the world, especially in nature and within individual souls. They trusted inner experience over external authority in the search for spiritual truth. Emerson envisioned a "universal spirituality" that would draw upon the spiritual insight of a variety of religious traditions, leaving behind doctrine and other elements of religion that did not directly promote spiritual experience. He was an avid student of Asian religions, and a lot of his spiritual vocabulary came from Hinduism. In his writings, he described a god he called the Over-Soul—an impersonal, infinite spiritual unity—and a universe that is continually emerging from this infinite, flowing spirit. In Emerson's cosmology, the material and the spiritual are levels of existence that correspond to each other, the spiritual generating the material and the material reflecting the spiritual. The divine is revealed in nature and in human experience, and human beings are meant to connect to and express divine energy.

Emerson's spirituality emphasized mysticism—direct spiritual experience. He encouraged people to cultivate a receptive state of mind to allow spontaneous insight to emerge. With an attitude of quiet receptivity to their own experience, people could experience themselves as connected, at their deepest levels, to the universal soul that unites all beings. The true self, according to Emerson, is not the body nor the ego nor the individual's social roles, but rather the self who has "become nothing"—become receptive to the instreaming power of the Over-Soul.[24]

The spirituality of Emerson and the Transcendental Club was philosophical; these were people interested in a worldview, a perspective on the nature of reality. In the decades following the Transcendental Club's emergence, other seekers developed spiritual systems that resonated with Transcendentalism but focused more concretely on what might be called technologies of the spirit—techniques for tapping into the constant flow of divine energy.

The New Thought movement, for example, began in the 1840s and emphasized the power of the mind to influence material reality. New Thought leaders believed that self-defeating beliefs and attitudes led to illness and limitation, and that people can change their health and their lives by changing their thoughts and connecting to a higher wisdom. The Spiritualist movement also began in the 1840s. Its leader, Andrew Jackson Davis, experienced himself as channeling the thoughts of spirit beings. He described the universe as a set of concentric spheres; divine energy flows from the higher, more spiritual spheres to lower, more material ones, and people can connect to the higher spheres for guidance. Davis's followers promoted the idea that the spheres between people and God are populated by angels and other spirit guides that people can contact for help, guidance, and comfort. In 1870, Helena Blavatsky founded the Theosophical Society. In Blavatsky's cosmology, people exist on seven levels from the gross physical body to subtler astral and etheric bodies, and each challenge a person faces is an opportunity for spiritual growth. Through Theosophy, Blavatsky brought many Hindu concepts into popular circulation, including reincarnation, karma, and chakras. She taught that people can become more receptive to spiritual energy by opening the chakras, seven spiritual energy centers inside the human body.

Transcendentalism, New Thought, Spiritualism, and Theosophy set the stage for a growing American interest in the world's religions, which helped bring about the first World's Parliament of Religions in Chicago in 1893. The Parliament included Hindu Swami Vivekananda, who went on to found the Vedanta Society; Anagarika Dharmapala, who later lectured widely about Theravada Buddhism; and Shaku Soyen, whose student D.T. Suzuki popularized Zen Buddhism in America. Also at the Parliament was Sarah Farmer, who was inspired to found Greenacre, a summer community in rural Maine dedicated to the comparative study of religions.

This history could be continued; these spiritual leaders, movements, events, and communities were followed by others equally noteworthy: American intellectuals such as William James, Carl Jung, Aldous Huxley, Huston

Smith, and Ken Wilber; Asian religious leaders such as Paramahansa Yogananda, Maharishi Mahesh Yogi, Shunryu Suzuki Roshi, and the fourteenth Dalai Lama; later World Parliaments of Religion in 1993, 1999, 2004, 2007, and 2009; and centers for spiritual education, including the California Institute of Integral Studies, Esalen, Kripalu Center, the Institute of Noetic Sciences, and Omega Institute for Holistic Studies.

In this history, we see seeds of some of the main themes of the current spirituality movement:

- The universe is imagined of in terms of corresponding layers, or levels. The spiritual energizes and informs the material, and the material reflects or refracts the spiritual, as a rainbow to white light.
- The divine is immanent: God is to be found in the world, in our own inner experience, in one another, and in nature. The divine is imagined using metaphors of energy, power, electricity, and light.
- People have a higher self that is connected to or one with the divine; we can cultivate this connection using practices that quiet the noise of the social world, allowing us to hear from this higher self.
- Spirituality involves a shift in perspective to a worldview that emphasizes meaning and interconnectedness. It also involves concrete practices designed to attune the mind to spiritual energies, higher planes of existence, or spirit beings; these practices promote overall health, well-being, and creativity.
- Spiritual life is about growth, development, and ongoing unfoldment; people can progress in their spiritual lives.
- A spiritual life requires openness to new experience and ideas and to a variety of religious symbols. The world's religions are resources that help us understand and express spiritual ideas rather than comprehensive traditions with ultimate authority. Judgments are based not on external authority, but on a pragmatic standard: What works? What facilitates spiritual growth and a spiritually attuned way of life?

The spirituality movement is diverse, and different ideas on this list have been emphasized and developed by different agents of it, including cognitive therapists; self-help writers; the New Age movement; new traditions such as Christian Science, the Unity Church, and Theosophy; Asian-inspired meditation movements; complementary medicine practitioners; and others. Meanwhile, these ideas in broad form remain part of the foundational repertoire of the mainstream spirituality movement.[25]

To the American spirituality movement, reflexive spirituality speaks of tradition. The spirituality movement was born of a frustration with America's dominant religious traditions. The Transcendentalists felt that the Christian churches of their day provided very limited resources for cultivating spirituality. Conservative Christianity was absorbed in legalisms and lists of beliefs, and liberal Christianity had become overrationalized, emphasizing progressive morality at the expense of the mystical and transcendent. Also, no matter how much liberal Christianity came to open itself to the wisdom of other religions, it was still Christianity, and the Transcendentalists and other spiritual seekers haven't always found what they needed in the Christian story or in Christian imagery and rituals.

When the Baby Boomers began to develop an unchurched spiritual culture, their anti-institutionalism and suspicion of tradition left much of the spirituality movement relatively disconnected from older religious traditions. The spirituality movement is *open* to different religions traditions, but not always particularly *engaged* with different religious traditions, including its own. Certainly some people who describe themselves as "spiritual but not religious" are learning about Buddhism or Judaism or Islam or Hinduism, but often they are only learning about one Buddhist meditation practice; or only about Kabbalah or Sufism, the mystical branches of Judaism and Islam; or about chakras, karma, and reincarnation only as they are understood in the American spirituality movement, not as they are understood in Hinduism. Many people who are spiritual but not religious have no sense at all that they are part of a 180-year-old American tradition that they could explore as they deepen their own spirituality.

With reflexive spirituality, seekers are approaching religious tradition again. Reflexive spirituality offers seekers a way to engage tradition without handing over their authority or pledging their allegiance to any particular tradition or institution. Reflexive spirituality is grounded in the tradition of the Transcendentalists and shares their value for individual autonomy, personal growth, mystical experience, transcendent awareness, openness, and wisdom. At the same time, reflexive spirituality is also grounded in intellectual traditions that offer tools for engaging with religion: tools of inquiry, of interpretation, of comparison, discernment, and discrimination. Reflexive seekers are using these tools to lend solidity, systematicity, and depth to their spiritual seeking. They are approaching religious traditions as archives of human wisdom, records of spiritual experience and insight that have been accumulated over millennia and around the world. They recognize that religious traditions don't need to be totally authoritative to be worthwhile. Reflexive spirituality makes religion more available to spiritual seekers and so offers resources that spirituality divorced from religion can't provide. With reflexive spirituality, spiritual seekers can engage religious traditions seriously, but on their own terms. In doing so, they can learn about the value of tradition, wrestle with each tradition's unique insights, and enrich their understanding of different traditions' shared wisdom.

3 THE TYRANNY OF THE TECHNICAL

There's an age-old urge to find the infinite
But the modern world of reason just negates this
And it leaves us with no substitutes at all . . .

—CHRIS CUNNINGHAM AND JOHNNY HERMANSON, *Crescent Moon*[1]

Reflexive spiritualists have a bone to pick with modern society. We've been taken over, they believe, by a kind of technical, means-ends thinking. What's the most efficient way to get from here to there? What do I have to do to reach my goals? How can I get more done? What are the correct procedures? How do I influence people or manipulate objects or set up systems to achieve results? Few of us would say that these are life's most important questions, but these are the questions that organize our society, certainly in the spheres of business and government, and increasingly in the rest of life. In the sphere of religion, too, we sometimes see this same emphasis on finding the best means to a given end: What do I have to believe to be saved? What do I have to do to get to heaven? An urban legend has it that while the Dalai Lama was on a U.S. speaking tour, an audience member asked him, "What's the quickest, easiest, most efficient way to get to enlightenment?" According to the story, the question made the Dalai Lama cry.

Reflexive spiritualists are equally frustrated with this kind of thinking, which scholars call *technical reason* or *technological rationality*. Technological rationality is a particular kind of rationality that emphasizes the calculated manipulation of the objective world according to impersonal rules and procedures. It's a means-ends logic that helps us identify the best steps to take to accomplish a particular goal, the kinds of goals that our existing resources will allow us to pursue, and the kinds of information we need to answer specific questions. Applied to the right kinds of problems, technological rationality can be our best friend. It can help us design buildings, fix cars, and find the best mode of transportation to get to our destination. It helps us set up scientific experiments, bureaucratic procedures, and investment portfolios. We use it to set goals and identify steps that will help us reach those goals. It's technological rationality that tells us that if we want to lose weight, we need to eat right and exercise, and it's technological rationality that's helping us decode the human genome.

The problem is that we overuse this kind of means-ends thinking—it's become our default way of approaching life. Technological rationality is a useful way of approaching many problems, but it's not so useful at helping us find meaning in life, and in fact, it can be a major obstacle to finding meaning in life. In their theories of modern society, both Jurgen Habermas and Anthony Giddens have touched on the role that technological rationality plays in draining the meaning out of modern culture. Habermas and Giddens think that formal systems that rely on predictability, calculability, and routine (such as the systems that structure corporations and governments) have become too powerful in modern societies, and they see technological rationality as an important part of these too-powerful systems.[2] And the hermeneutic philosopher Paul Ricoeur made technological rationality a centerpiece of his theory of how meaninglessness has become a problem for modern societies. Ricoeur argued that when this kind of reason becomes too powerful, it limits people's ability to interpret life poetically—it leads us to see literal, concrete realities as the only true realities.[3]

The people of First United Methodist Church, Common Ground, and the other settings I observed didn't use the terms "technological rationality" or "technical reason." But they often expressed frustration with elements of modern culture that make meaning hard to find, and the things that frustrated them were all related to technological rationality. Reflexive spiritualists criticized modern culture for emphasizing the literal, the material, the right rules, and the correct procedures. They were frustrated by what they saw as an American eagerness to jump to conclusions, to look for the one certain answer and the one right way—and to get there quickly. This kind of thinking, they argued, keeps us focused on the surfaces of life and makes us impatient with complexity. Life becomes all about achieving goals, finding solutions, and arriving at definitive answers. We can't get at the deeper meanings of life with this kind of thinking. In fact, if this is our habitual mode of thought, the whole idea of deep meanings may not make sense to us.

For reflexive spiritualists, it's as though we've become a nation of Joe Fridays running around asking for "just the facts, ma'am"—afraid to waste time, unwilling to consider anything outside the horizon of verifiable fact, and determined to stay on track so we can wrap up the case and go home. This approach to life may help us cross items off our to-do lists, but it cuts deeper meaning off at the root. How can we explore the transcendent, the mysterious, the ineffable, the wise, within the constraints of a "Dragnet" approach to life?

Technological rationality is like a lens or a filter we can use to look at life. I have light eyes, and on a bright day, my view of the world changes when I put on sunglasses. Without sunglasses, I see the rich, bright colors of the sky and trees and grass, but the brightness of the sun keeps me from seeing finer details. When I put on sunglasses, colors become muted, but I can make out the texture of the clouds. Technological reason is kind of like that: like all epistemologies and worldviews, it helps us see some aspects of reality, but obscures other aspects of reality. And if we think that reality is only what we can see through the lens of technological rationality, then we're missing out on other aspects of reality that matter if we want to experience life as meaningful.

What technological rationality obscures is the transcendent. According to reflexive spiritualists, the patterns of technological rationality train our attention in ways that make spiritual realities difficult to even imagine, let alone perceive. To put it baldly, technical reason hides God from us. By definition, transcendent reality—God, the divine, spiritual truth, wisdom, deeper meaning—lies beyond the concrete, the literal, the technical, and the practical. We can't see spiritual realities when we're focusing on technical procedures and lifeless facts. The transcendent just doesn't fit into those parameters. But we don't have to be limited by technological rationality. There are other ways of seeing life, other lenses we can use, that make the transcendent easier to see.

The reflexive spiritualists I observed had four main criticisms of modern culture, or what I'm calling technical reason. Their first three criticisms are about surfaces and depths. Technical reason naturally focuses people's attention on life's surfaces—literal meanings, material realities, and procedural rules and routines. But the transcendent is profound. Trying to fit the transcendent into a framework that only understands the literal, the material, and the procedural is like trying to squeeze three dimensions into two. Their fourth criticism has to do with what might be called "closure." Technical reason encourages us to come to solid conclusions based on established facts—but the transcendent is mysterious and ever-evolving. It can't be captured by unalterable statements of fact; it requires an openness to complexity, unpredictability, and surprise.

This chapter discusses each of these four criticisms in turn. I describe how reflexive spiritualists talked about these four patterns of technical reason, why they found them frustrating, and what they proposed as alternatives.

Literalism: Too Small for Transcendence

I've seen diamonds shining away
On a golden ocean's glitter
And people living every day
As if all it is is water

—CHRIS CUNNINGHAM AND JOHNNY HERMANSON, *I am a Lover*[4]

The literal meaning of anything is its surface meaning—its most obvious, apparent meaning, or as Webster's says, its ordinary, factual meaning. Any statement, action, or word can have only one literal meaning—the correct one. Literal language is useful because it allows us to make statements of fact. When we speak literally, we're drawing simple and clear correspondences between words and facts, so that when we hear, for example, that water molecules are composed of two hydrogen atoms and one oxygen atom, we can assume that we're hearing an accurate description of the reality of water. But this is a very different description of water than we hear from poets and songwriters. Which is more true? Which is more real?

Reflexive spiritualists are clear on this question: truth isn't always about fact, and the most important truths can't be reduced to fact. But our society values fact more than it values other kinds of truth, and so we're focused on literalism. In a technologically rational society, if something isn't factual—isn't true *literally*—then it can't be true at all. Or at best, it can be somehow "less true" than facts are—a watered-down version of the truth, or a flowery embellishment of the truth.[5] This narrowing of the definition of truth frustrates reflexive spiritualists because it makes it hard to recognize deeper truths—the kinds of truths that are more important, more meaningful, than facts can ever be.

As I listened to reflexive spiritualists in different kinds of settings, I heard them criticize literalism over and over. But this criticism was of special importance in religious settings. Conservative Christianity, and especially Protestant fundamentalism, has held up literalism as the only valid approach to the Bible. But nonreligious people also often assume that literalism is the only way to interpret religious texts, and consequently wonder how people could ever believe what their religions are telling them. To reflexive Christians, literalism seemed not only mistaken, but also *loud*. It seemed to them that most people weren't even aware of the possibility and potential of nonliteralist approaches to religious texts. As a result, reflexive Christians gave a lot of attention to the problem of literalism. The leaders and members of First United Methodist Church, for example, often spoke against literalism in what sometimes sounded like a one-sided argument with fundamentalist Christianity. In one sermon, pastor David spoke at length about the difference between literalism and truth, and encouraged his congregation to look beyond literalism to consider the Bible's deeper meanings:

> The heart of being a Christian is an event—Jesus's life—and that event's *impact*, *meaning* for you and me, and that's *interpretation*, not description. The Gospels are not so much descriptive as they are interpretive.
>
> If I had had the time and resources for this sermon, I would have brought up various artists' paintings of Jesus—we'd see they'd all be different. In some Jesus would be a blond Scandinavian, in some he would be an Irish shepherd, in some he would have Oriental features, in some he would have dark skin and dark hair as if he was from Africa, in some he would appear as a Middle Eastern peasant. They would all be different.
>
> Having seen that, I hope you wouldn't ask, "So which one is real, what did Jesus really look like?" Because to ask that question is to miss the reason why the artist painted the picture, which was to say, "This is the impact Jesus has on me." The artist wasn't trying to say, "Here's what Jesus looked like"; it wasn't a photographic attempt. The artist was saying, "In him I find the fullness of my humanity, and I learn more about God. I want to show you this so that you might find that too."
>
> So too with the Gospels. The Gospels are not a literal history. They are an interpretation of the meaning of Jesus for the Gospelwriters. They were written for religious instruction, not for historical description. The Gospels have an agenda. John is up front about it: "These are written that you may believe that Jesus is the Christ, the Son of God, and that believing, you may have life in his name" (John 20:31). The creeds are saying, "This is what he means to me," and that ends with the question, "What does he mean to you?" The creeds are interpretations.

Similarly, Cecil's Sunday School classes were often punctuated with conversations like this one:

BETTY: The Bible is parable, allegory, and mythology.
COLIN: Can you have a philosophy of life it's just all made up?
CECIL: Can we have a Christian approach to the world without taking the Bible literally? I say yes, I think we must take the Bible seriously, but not literally. If someone says to me, "I need to believe that Jesus literally turned water into wine to have faith," I don't want to say anything to undermine that, to undermine their faith. But for me, I don't need to believe that to have faith.

For reflexive spiritualists, religious literalism takes the meaning out of religion. I heard this criticism in nonreligious settings, too. During a Common Ground event, for example, a small group of people were talking about their religious upbringing. Charles said he was brought up Catholic, and said to me, "The Catholic church literalized the metaphors of the trinity, the Son of God, all that, so that your generation finds it all meaningless." And during a radio interview, religious historian Huston Smith described literalism as the *least* meaningful way to interpret scriptures. Smith was speaking of the rise of religious fundamentalism; he described it as a "digging in" response to perceived threats from modern intellectualism:

And their mistake was to dig in on literalism. Which will not work all the way. Actually, in all the great religions, there is a very sophisticated tradition of exegesis, interpretation of the scriptures. And in the Christian view, it has four levels.

First, you begin with the *literal* meaning of the text, but that's the lowest; next the *ethical* meaning, next the *allegorical* meaning, and finally, the *anagogical* meaning. I wonder if you even know that word! I wonder how many of our listeners know the word "anagogic"! ["Anagogic" means] does it *inspire* you. And that's the top principle! So the fundamentalists have dug in their heels on the literal interpretation, which will not give an adequate true message, the message of the tradition in question.

For reflexive spiritualists, religious literalism makes religion less meaningful than it can otherwise be. But they don't see religious literalism as the only kind of literalism that plagues modern society. Outside of Christian settings, reflexive spiritualists talked about literalism not just as a religious problem, but also as a broad cultural trend. During a Common Ground weekend retreat, for example, Jim talked about the idea of magic. Jim thought that the idea of magic could be a powerful, meaningful idea, but not if we take it too literally:

JIM: There's the holistic, community way of deeper understanding and en-riching life, and the fundamentalist way. The fundamentalist way is to say, "We have the wrong rock" or "Today's Thursday, it should be amethyst." Aromatherapy is an egregious example of assertion rather than teaching.

Some cultures do this in a context, it's a "Let's explore the possibilities together." We live in a culture where assertion of one-to-one correspond-ence is all over. In Freudian dream interpretation books, you look up a symbol and it says "that means this." Jungian dream interpretation books are different. Jung says to understand a dream, you have to "play the myth onward." I believe in the power of symbols in the context of conscious soul work to enrich life.

RON: I have a lot of resistance to "magic"; I associate it with cheap grace.

JIM: That's the fundamentalist association of the power with the thing.

At another Common Ground event, Wayne spoke about the spiritual rich-ness of nature. He said, "Ancient people look at a river and ask, 'What does it mean?' Modern people have no idea it means anything—we've lost our capac-ity to ask." And in a public radio interview, anthropologist Vincent Crapan-zano compared religious literalism to the literalism he found in legal and sci-entific talk:

There's a propensity that we have in this country . . . to try and find that single commonsensical meaning that a word has, and by extension, particular kinds of phenomena, like the gene in the sense of "there's a gene for it," so that explains it totally.

In all these examples, people are criticizing strictly literal interpretations of objects in the world—the Bible, dreams, rivers, oceans, human biology— for being too simplistic, for being concerned only with simple surface corre-spondences, for focusing too much on simple denotation. What all this lit-eralism obscures is the possibility of *connotation*: life's symbolic value; the potential of every object, event, and story to reveal profound meaning. To look at the world literally—to see only apparent, surface meanings—is to miss most of the picture, because by its very nature, transcendent meaning lies beyond the kinds of simple surface correlations that Jim called "one-to-one correspondences." As Cecil said to his Theology for the Twenty-First Century class, "For me, it's axiomatic that the word God refers to something too big for me to get my mind around. I have a feeling that I experience in poetry, and I only have a few pale phrases of prose to express it."

Because the transcendent is "too big" for literal interpretation, reflexive spiritualists encouraged each other to look at scriptures and at the world in a different way. The perspective they encouraged was what sociologist Robert Bellah once called "symbolic realism" and what Cecil called "taking symbols seriously but not literally."[6] They wanted people to adopt a metaphorical consciousness—a habit of looking for multiple layers of significance and a readiness to see deeper and deeper meanings. Literalism limits us to one single correct meaning. But a metaphorical perspective gives every word, story, and object an ever-expanding array of meanings. So Common Ground teacher Wayne, for example, encouraged his students to see nature metaphorically:

> There are intrinsic meanings in nature. Nature tells a story about creation. . . . An exegesis is where you take a Biblical text and pull out the meaning of it. You can do an exegesis with a rose. . . . Allow yourself to see at a deeper level. The divine is like an artist. The rose, every being, is like a treatise on creation, *if we know how to look!*

Jim told his students, "Myth, religion, and dreams are all related. . . . Learning to think symbolically is the key to understanding all of these." At First Church, Cecil encouraged his classes to use a metaphorical perspective to find deeper meaning in the Bible, advising them to "think about the poetry of these stories." He told the Theology for the Twenty-First Century class, "The future of Christian faith rests not on reasserting human doctrines, but on refashioning the symbols. We'll need those symbols, analogies, metaphors, but we'll need to use them in a way that we *realize* we're using a metaphor."

Gregg Levoy, author of *Callings: Finding and Following an Authentic Life*, leads workshops on following a professional or other life calling. During a workshop I attended, he told participants that they could find meaning by taking a metaphorical approach to life in general. He introduced the program by saying:

> This workshop is about the search for signs that will bring you into alignment with your purpose, your mission. I compare it to tracking

animals; we're tracking signs. Cultivate enthusiasm for the hunt, and your life will show you things it wouldn't otherwise. Joseph Campbell said the great sacrilege, in terms of the soul's integrity, is inadvertence. Not paying attention to the signs, not being awake. . . . Suddenly, you see all these new signs, that were there before, but now you're seeing them. To me, part of the key is *looking* for meaning.

Physical symptoms . . . for example, if you have a stiff neck constantly. In addition to treating the symptoms—in addition to treating the symptoms—ask the metaphoric questions: "Is there a way in which I feel rigid in my life?" My brother, who is a real type A personality, got a hernia. I asked him how he got it, and he said he was on the toilet, and he was pushing too hard! I thought, pushing too hard, yep. He's a classic pusher. Insomnia—is there a way some part of me wants to wake up? You can get harebrained about asking these kinds of questions too, but they're worth asking.

Vincent Crapanzano and his interviewer, Jean Feraca, also advocated metaphor as a solution to the limiting nature of literalism:

FERACA: We should teach poetry, because if you study poetry, you become much more comfortable with ambiguity.

CRAPANZANO: I totally agree, and the phrase "comfortable with ambiguity" is extremely important, because that's ultimately what's at stake here, is the fact that we're living in a world that is incredibly ambiguous, and that we have to learn to live with that.

FERACA: The opposite of literal thinking is—

CRAPANZANO: Figurative. At one point I thought of a title for the book, my editor didn't like it, called "Fear of Figuration." And what I really meant was that there was a real fear of the possibility of this kind of poetic, this kind of nonliteral, this kind of creative thinking.

FERACA: The ability to make metaphors, after all, is the best antidote to literalism.

What are we missing if we think that *truth* and *fact* mean the same thing? According to reflexive spiritualists, what we're missing is everything that's most important: "the fullness of humanity," "inspiration," "richness of life," "deep understanding," "creativity"—transcendent meaning.

Scientism: The Transcendent Lies Beyond the Five Senses

It is a science with a limited scope,
Where the heart and head collide,
Resigned to the laws of only tangible proof
To which the truth does not abide.
We stifle
And smother
The mystic wonder.
Is our arrogance a deafening fear of what we'll have to hear? . . .
We have a tendency to think that it's our practical senses
That get these questions solved.
But those are tenuous tools, and the more we employ them,
The slower we evolve.
Denied by our suppression, the deeper lessons.

—STUART DAVIS, *Universe Communion*[7]

The best definition of *scientism* comes from world religions scholar Huston Smith: Scientism is a worldview that holds "first, that the scientific method is, if not the only reliable method of getting at truth, then at least the most reliable method; and second, that the things science deals with—material entities—are the most fundamental things that exist."[8] Scientism takes science and makes a kind of god out of it, treating it as the last word on reality.

Reflexive spiritualists criticize scientism for the same reasons that they criticize literalism. They think that literalism reduces our view of reality—that it leads us to believe that things have to be factual to be true, or that facts are somehow "more true" than symbols and metaphors are. Reflexive spiritualists believe the opposite—that the truths that metaphors reveal are often more important, more fundamental, and more meaningful than facts are. In the same way, reflexive spiritualists believe that scientism reduces our view of reality—it leads us to believe that reality is nothing more than the material world, or that the material world is somehow "more real" than the transcendent or spiritual world. And again, reflexive spiritualists tend to believe the opposite—that transcendent reality, spiritual reality, is the foundation of life, and that material reality is secondary.

The reflexive spiritualists I observed were not hostile to science—in fact, a couple of them were natural scientists themselves. They just believed that science is a *limited* way of learning about the world, one that can't tell us about realities that go beyond what we can observe with our senses. They didn't want us to limit our understanding of reality to the things that science can show us—in other words, to the material world that we observe with our senses. For reflexive spiritualists, there's simply more to reality than meets the eye, and that "more" is what matters most of all.

To make this point, reflexive spiritualists distinguished what we can know scientifically from what can only be understood metaphorically. For example, during Lent, First United Methodist Church hosted Wednesday night discussions featuring a video series called "Jesus: The New Way." One of these videos featured a discussion of whether the resurrection of Jesus could be verified historically. Shortly before this Wednesday, pastor David had given sermons that criticized approaches to Christianity that emphasized historical accuracy rather than symbolic truth. This was early in my research at First Church, and I wondered if David's perspective was shared by others in the church, so, during the discussion after the video, I asked Joan, First Church's associate pastor, a question:

KELLY: I was thinking about the sermons of the last couple weeks, and David saying that to ask what really happened was to ask the wrong question. How does that jibe with this?

JOAN: I think David's sermons and this video are both running into the same phenomenon, which is our twentieth-century scientific mindset, where we consider truth to be what we can observe with our senses, and nothing else can be truth. So David is saying to ask what really happened historically is to ask the wrong question, and I agree with that, but this video is saying if we're gonna do that, let's at least look at the history and the context and see what we can and can't know. So they're coming at the same thing from two different angles.

Joan wasn't putting down scientific history. In fact, she was saying that because it's valuable, it's important to do it right. But for Joan, David, and other reflexive spiritualists, scientific history doesn't have what it takes to get at transcendent truths. At a Common Ground event, Wayne made a similar comment about the limits of science and expressed optimism that scientism is on the decline:

What we're seeing now is a slow breakdown of the hold science had on culture. People no longer see science as the only way to know. Soon we'll see a congeniality developing . . . rather than naïve realism, material reductionism, it's all just objective.

Scientism came up explicitly during a Common Ground discussion of violence and people who commit mass violence. Evan brought up the possibility that mass murderers may be suffering from physiological problems, and others in the group were quick to point to the limits of that way of under-standing violence:

EVAN: What about brain research? There are all these physiological things that affect people . . .

RON: I think of it like a circle, and you can enter the circle at different places. Sometimes a chemical is an avenue, but I don't think chemical treatment by itself is a solution.

TERESA: Chemical treatment might stop a person's more violent impulses, but it won't solve the violence in society.

JIM: We're such a scientistic culture. We take science *so* seriously, we imagine that it's the final answer, and now science has spoken on this topic, so that invalidates all other perspectives from the history of the humanities. . . . I think there's a huge mistake in the scientistic view that once an organic component has been identified, the *cause* has been found. All you can say is there's a correspondence . . . there is an organic aspect. There's an organic manifestation of meditation. But it's a *complex*.

In a public lecture I attended as part of my field work, Huston Smith told the audience that scientism leads us to limit what we think of as "real" to the pa-rameters of what science can detect:

> Up to the rise of modern science, all people lived under a religious view of reality, characterized by an acknowledgment of transcendence—a realm of reality that exceeds the physical universe. The world's reli-gions speak *with one voice* to the thesis that there is more than the physical universe we pick up with our senses.
>
> If there is anything greater than we are—angels, extraterrestrials, God—we have no idea how those superior intelligences work, and so there's no way we can mount a controlled experiment to see if they're there or not. We're like a pack of dogs saying, "We keep hearing there is something called mathematics. Is there? Let's put it to the test. We'll put it to the Sniff Test."

As Smith's comparison implies, there's a touch of hubris to scientism—the arrogance of believing that our perceptions form the limits of what can be real. But by definition, the transcendent *transcends* our ordinary observation. So to experience reality as transcendently meaningful, we need to be open to the possibility that there may be important realities that we can't detect with science. In a scientistic culture, this idea is suspect, and so spirituality is suspect, as two women in First Church's Faith and Reason group observed one day:

CAROL: Science is embodied; we observe through our senses. Religion says
we're not just body; we're also spirit, and we can't use our senses to measure
spirit. Maybe we can observe spirit, but we're not aware of it enough to try.
DONNA: Or if spiritual things do pop up, we're so trained to disbelieve, that
we discount them.

The problem, according to reflexive spiritualists, is that the realities that we may be missing, that we're "trained to disbelieve," are the ones that give deeper meaning to our lives. Author Wayne Dyer made this argument in a televised talk called "Improving Your Life Using the Wisdom of the Ages":

So many of us are separated from our source. Through the ego, through
this identification with all the stuff that's out there happening. And so
many of these teachers spoke about this quality of the soul, this quality
of the spirit, this quality of being more than just what you notice, this
quality of being more than just what you observe.

Dyer is pointing to the limits that scientism places on our sense of self. He's contrasting a scientistic, technologically rational view of the human being, defined by observable physical reality, with a spiritual view of the human being as something greater than that.

"There's more to life than material reality" was the core of reflexive spiritualists' criticism of scientism, but their critique got more complex than that. We've developed whole systems of thought to help us understand and organize material reality—not only the natural sciences, but also the social sciences, including law and economics. These systems of thought help us make sense of material reality, but they don't transfer well to spiritual reality, and relying on them out of habit can make it hard to think meaningfully about spirituality. So, for example, in one Common Ground class, Wayne was discussing the spiritual concept of the oneness of humanity. He told his students that they would be able to understand this idea better if they temporarily set aside materialist categories of thought:

Everything is mediated through consciousness, and there's only one
consciousness; the divine is all of it, and we're all in it. . . . So self, soul,

the person, *is* the community of consciousness, individually experienced and appropriated. Each of us is consciousness from a particular perspective. To understand this, we have to let go of the ownership principle, which is a legal, economic category, not a spiritual category.

Consultant Jack Shea made the same kind of point during a workshop with business people about bringing spirituality to work. The concept of accumulation, he argued, helps us organize material reality, but gets in the way of understanding spiritual reality:

> Spiritual traditions are often contrary, unconventional ways of thinking. One of the things they think is misguided, is that we think development takes place by doing more—accumulation. They think more and more makes us cluttered. Do less, and your essence or soul shines forth.... Doing less can access more of you.

The philosopher Paul Ricoeur wrote that modern culture has created "the prejudice that reality is only what is manipulatable."[9] He thought that if we were to bring meaning back into modern society, we would need to "deconstruct . . . the assurances of modern man" and "struggle with the believable and unbelievable of our time in order to make a place for intelligent discourse."[10] Jack Shea, Common Ground's Wayne, and other reflexive spiritualists agree: scientism is a prejudice that makes it hard to understand spiritual wisdom, hard to notice spiritual realities, and hard to even imagine that spirituality could be real.

Rules and Routine: Purpose, Not Procedure

Red tape. Standard procedure. Bureaucracy. The proper channels. Regulation. The letter of the law. What do these phrases call to mind? How do they feel? To reflexive spiritualists, they connote mindless routine, purposeless rules, and empty procedure: meaninglessness. Modern culture, they believe, relies too much on rules and routines, and in our dependence, we easily lose sight of the original meanings, true intentions, or deeper purposes of the rules and routines that we follow. Even worse, we get used to approaching life as a simple set of causes and effects: If I do *x*, then *y* will happen. If I follow the rules, then I will be okay. The important thing is to find out what I'm supposed to do and then do that. And if I want to help others, the best thing I can do is tell them what to do—offer them a set of rules to live by. Once again, our attention is focused on life's surfaces—correct behaviors and required procedures—rather than its depths.

It was this sense of shallowness—emptiness—that most frustrated reflexive spiritualists. For example, reflexive Christians criticized the way the afterlife was often discussed in religious circles. It seemed to them that many religious people spoke of the afterlife mostly as a reward or punishment for good behavior. To reflexive spiritualists, this approach to the afterlife is morally bereft. At First Church, for example, the Theology for the Twenty-First Century class spent several months working through the book *Why the Church Must Change or Die*, by Episcopal Bishop John Shelby Spong. Cecil opened one class by asking the group to reflect on Spong's comments on the afterlife:

CECIL: Spong says, "The hope for life after death must be separated forever from the reward-and-punishment mentality the church has used to keep people in line." I want to explore what we think of life after death and heaven and hell. What do we think about using hell as a behavior-control device? What do you really think about life after death, hell, heaven? On a personal level, my father died some years ago; what do I think about that with respect to him?

JUDY: We're spirit, the spirit lives on, the body dies.

CECIL: The spirit lives on and the body dies. And does that do it for us?

SEVERAL PEOPLE: No!

JERRY: It's a quid pro quo, a business deal—do this and you'll get this, don't do that and you'll get that, automatic, because those are the conditions of the deal. If it's just a deal, what is the spiritual content of that?

CECIL: So you're saying it's morally equivalent to you put your quarters in and you get your Coke.

CAROL: It makes it all selfish, so that you're being kind to others so you can get to heaven, not because you love your neighbor.

Cecil, Jerry, and Carol—along with Spong—saw the reward-and-punishment approach to the afterlife as spiritually empty, shallow, and meaningless. What meaning is there, they ask, in just following the rules to get the reward? The problem, for reflexive spiritualists, is not that the rules are too strict—that they ask too much of people. The problem is that "following the rules" doesn't ask *enough* of people—and doesn't give much back. Carol, for example, thinks spirituality should help people cultivate genuine love for others—the kind of love that would make kindness toward others natural and genuine rather than artificial and selfish.

Over in the Faith and Reason group, Alan made a similar criticism, this time focused on Christian fundamentalism: "Fundamentalists are abdicating responsibility—'I'll follow the rules and I'll get to heaven.'" Janet, who worked with high-school students, agreed with Alan, saying, "I ask my students, if it could be proved that there is no God, would you change your life? Consistently, it's the fundamentalist students, and only them, who say absolutely, they would stop being a good person, because they're counting on that reward." A man named Stan called in to Wisconsin Public Radio during Winifred Gallagher's interview to make the same point: he said, "Life after death has been the most fundamental principle in the Judeo-Christian tradition. There's no point in being good unless it earns you the right to heaven." Alan, Janet, and Stan thought that when religions focus on behavioral rules, they breed shallow, irresponsible, selfish believers.

At Common Ground, Ron told his students that behavioral rules are just one half of a spiritual truth, and that if they only focused on following the rules, they would miss deeper truths. You can't really get at the spiritual value of religious rules, according to Ron, unless you also experience a deep, ongoing connection with the transcendent:

> People turn away from religion because they simply feel they've been given rules. Paul Tillich said, "I don't want to obey rules from a stranger, even if the stranger is God." It's the intimacy with the divine, the radical amazement at the divine, that makes sense of this feeling of being commanded.
>
> This is what's the problem with the New Age. People go from weekend to weekend looking for spiritual highs; they get their highs, and they go home. That's not spirituality. Spirituality is action in the world, *and* a connection to the divine. These must be connected, integrated. If they're separated, you get false paths. You either get ethical laws without any experience to make sense of them, or you get this high without any action in the world.

In themselves, Ron is saying, ethical rules are meaningless. They only make sense in the context of something much deeper—an intimate connection with the divine.

The same is true of empty routine. When reflexive spiritualists criticized rules, they were usually talking about religious life. When they criticized routine, they were often talking about secular life. But both religious rules and secular routines have the same spirit-numbing effect, in their eyes. Criticisms of empty routine were especially common in the spirit-at-work movement. During one of Jack Shea's lunchtime programs on spirituality at work, business people compared work routines to religious rules and spoke of spirituality as the life-giving antidote to both:

SCOTT: People get tied up with religious rules. You can't eat meat on Friday, you can't do this, you must do that; people associate religion with rules. A partner at work is like that—if you don't do that rule, forget it, you're going to hell. Spirituality is less about rules, it's less, you're doomed if you don't follow the rules. That's the difference between religion and spirituality.

BETH: Dogma.

MICHAEL: I once looked up "spirit," and of course it comes from "espiritu," which means breath, or life. Some people are talking about organizations as living systems, rather than as machines. Spirit at work, we need to see work organizations as different from a machine. If it's a machine, we don't need breath, life. If it's a living system, it needs life.

JACK: In his book, Greg [Pierce, *Spirituality@Work: 10 Ways to Balance Your Life on the Job*] tells about a Jewish doctor who says a Jewish prayer every time she washes her hands. It's a purification prayer, but she's made it her own; she says it every time she washes her hands to remind her that the next person she meets is not their disease. Because her challenge is, instead of people, it becomes a series of maladies that she goes from room to room to see.

Greg Pierce, the author Jack referred to, was later interviewed by *Fortune* magazine, where he summed up the spirituality-at-work movement's criticism of empty routine by saying, "I like to think of us as the anti-Dilberts."[11]

For reflexive spiritualists, rules and routines are what happen when you take a transcendent realization and try to put it into technical, rational terms. Rules and routines are the rationalized sediment of genuine spiritual experience, an attempt to solidify and make practical a genuine insight. An experience of oneness with all creation, for example, might get translated into a rule about being kind to others, a prohibition against theft and murder, or a routine of almsgiving. Obviously, rules and routines like these aren't bad—it's just that, for reflexive spiritualists, they're not what matters most. Rules and routines exist to help people act on and remain conscious of deeper spiritual insights—deeper transcendent meanings. They're secondary to the more fundamental reality of the transcendent, and to see them as ends in themselves is once again to miss most of the story.

So reflexive spiritualists offered a different perspective. Instead of seeing rules and routines as ends in themselves, reflexive spiritualists encouraged one another to look for the original purposes or intentions behind the rules and routines of their lives. They encouraged one another to see those deeper purposes or intentions as more fundamental than the rules and routines themselves. For example, at Common Ground, Ron encouraged his students to consider the original mission of their organization, the purpose of their profession, the heart of their religion, and the experiences that sparked their interest in their current pursuits:

> In any organization, look at the organization's founding documents. What did we start out to do, what is this all about? In education—it's about *learning*. I had a student once who was so afraid of failing my class that he was unable to learn anything. So I met with him and told him that I would guarantee that he would pass my class. After that, he could relax and actually learn rather than worrying about failing.
>
> We have to remember what it's all about. In medicine, it's about healing, not about seeing the maximum number of patients and filling out insurance forms. In religion, it's about the experience of the divine, not about following the letter of the law. We have to keep going back. An astronomer has to *keep looking at the sky*.
>
> We have to go back to that fundamental experience. What is *life* fundamentally about? Experiencing the divine! Stay with that.

Wayne made the same point by telling a story about routines of dress in a Franciscan convent:

> I was consulting with some Franciscan nuns who had asked me to come in and advise them on some things, and one of the things we talked about was their dress. They were still wearing the old brown robes. And I said to them, "Look at the original reason why you dress this way. The founders of your tradition dressed this way to dress like the poor of that day. Now the poor don't dress like that anymore; your dress is not doing what it is supposed to be doing for you—putting you on a level with the poor people you serve."

Reflexive spiritualists want us to look beneath our daily routines, our religious rules, and our ordinary pursuits to see their deeper meaning. When we reconnect with these deeper meanings, we might see fit to make changes to our rules and routines so that they better reflect their real purposes. In the end, though, spiritual life shouldn't be an endless quest to perfect our rules and routines and then follow them, as they say, "religiously." For reflexive spiritualists, spiritual life is about those deeper meanings themselves—the deeper meanings that, as Ron said, come from "intimacy with the divine."

Closure: The Transcendent Can't Be Pinned Down

"What's the right answer? How soon can this be finished? What's the best solution? Can we get some hard data on this? What's your final answer?" These are the questions of a society preoccupied with what I call *closure*—an ends-orientation that inflates the value of conclusions and finality. Closure means bringing things to a close, and a value for closure makes us eager to bring all open questions to a close—to arrive at final answers, definitive conclusions, and expedient solutions. Reflexive spiritualists think modern culture is too focused on closure—too eager for answers, facts, the already known, and the unshakably certain. The transcendent, by contrast, is mysterious, complex, and continually evolving—it can't be pinned down with "final answers." Reflexive spiritualists worry that a society focused on closure will produce minds that can't stay open long enough to fully inquire into the deep possibility of the transcendent. By insisting on definitive conclusions, reflexive spiritualists argue, we miss out on the richness of life that accompanies a genuine ongoing engagement with transcendent meaning.

First Church members often seemed to me to be arguing with unseen Christian fundamentalists, and their critique of closure had that quality, too. Cecil, for example, told the Faith and Reason group that closure was one of the main differences between progressive Christianity and fundamentalist Christianity:

> There's some historical kernel [to the Bible], but it's not marked, "This is historical, this is mythological, this is allegory." Fundamentalists are better at giving answers. Someone said to me at a church where I was pastor, "This is different from my previous church. They had all the answers; you help us learn what the questions are." We don't specialize in sure and pat answers, but we are into questioning together.

For Cecil and other reflexive spiritualists, "questioning together" is what communal spiritual life is all about. Religions that claim to have "all the answers" are really forestalling genuine spirituality by bringing inquiry to an artificial close. The Common Ground leaders shared this opinion. Ron, for example, often criticized what he called "getting cozy" with whatever beliefs and practices we find most familiar or attractive:

> The ways we hold back, shut down, limit our world, solidify our world. There's a premature closure often—"let's get settled." Moses was called to lead the Exodus at eighty. Monks don't retire; they just die. Can I stop my spiritual life now? No! There has to be a commitment to hang in there. Don't run away from the pain of seeing yourself. It unnerves us, clear seeing without pushing away what you dislike, or getting cozy with what you find attractive. This is like cultic groups that want to have all the truths in their pocket, and they shut down.

Both Cecil and Ron saw spirituality as a continual process of growth and learning; to cut this process short is to stunt spiritual life.

For people who practice reflexive spirituality, the transcendent is simply too large and complex to be pinned down with what they called "easy answers"—or even with more complex theological answers. David put it this way during a Sunday sermon:

> We never find in the faith journey all the answers. . . . The divine is larger than any human language. We can't confine the divine to any one philosophy. Uncertainty is always there, ambiguity is always there. Beware of people who tell you they have all the answers. I'm most suspicious of them. It is not possible to have all the answers. What is important is not what we know, but our sincerity in the questions we are asking and our openness to hearing what God says in response.

In the theology of reflexive spirituality, the transcendent—the divine, God, the "something more"—defies definition. It can't be fenced in, pinned down—or put in a box. The "final word" doesn't exist, and never can exist. So reflexive spiritualists turned away from the search for answers, and turned toward an attitude of open inquiry and permanent questioning. Author Neale Donald Walsch, citing Sir John Templeton, called this stance "humility theology." In a public lecture, he told this story:

> I talked with Sir John Templeton, who created the Templeton prize in religion. I asked him, "If one thing could save us from the horror, what would it be?" He said, "Humility theology." Sir John Templeton is a

very conservative guy. This is not a New Age hippie. He has conservative politics and a conservative theology. But he thought the one thing that could save us would be a humility theology; a theology that would grant the possibility that it does not have all the answers, but just all the *questions*.

Common Ground teacher Jim told his students that an attitude of open-ended questioning is essential for drawing out the full possibilities of spiritual resources. He wrapped up a talk about the Taoist *I Ching* with these parting words:

> The way to phrase questions to the *I Ching* isn't "Should I do this or this? Yes or No?" It's "I'm deeply concerned about this." If a person goes to the *I Ching* looking for an answer, they'll find it frustrating. If a person goes to the *I Ching* looking for a new way to think about a question, they'll find it intriguing.

For Jim, the purpose of consulting the *I Ching* or any religious text is not to find answers, but to find insight, new perspective, and tools to feed reflection.

Author Danah Zohar, in a public radio interview, told listeners that this preoccupation with closure isn't just a religious problem—it's a broad cultural problem. Like other reflexive spiritualists, she wanted us to open our minds to the unknown, the uncertain, and the unpredictable:

> We as a culture tend to prefer answers to questions. . . . A lot of my life is spent lecturing to big corporations about their intelligence and their thinking processes, and there too I say, you know, you're far too answer-oriented; you stress what's known, what's certain, what's predictable. Go for the uncertainty, go for the questions, go for what you don't know. And that opens the brain up and opens the intelligence up. . . . The great rabbi Abraham Heschel, one of the great Jewish mystics of the twentieth century, said we're closer to God when we're asking questions than when we think we know the answers.

As Zohar's words suggest, it's a fallacy to believe that religions are made up of people who think they have all the right answers. Rabbi Heschel is far from the only prominent religious leader to promote the spiritual value of open-ended inquiry. But in a society that values hard facts, definitive knowledge, and expedient solutions, it's easy to bypass inquiry in both secular and religious life. In doing so, according to reflexive spiritualists, we not only cut short the possibilities for meaning—we actually bypass God.

Literalism, scientism, rules and routine, and closure are perfect for a society that values technological rationality. Literalism makes meaning obvious and static; it allows us to get on with achieving our goals without stopping to contemplate nuances of meaning. Scientism allows us to focus on the material world so that we know what to manipulate to achieve our goals. By creating and following rules and routines, we don't have to constantly invent new ways of getting things done. And by pursuing closure, we ensure that we do get things done. But transcendent meaning isn't an outcome of efficiency; it isn't a goal to reach or a task to accomplish. As the reflexive spiritualists in this chapter have argued, the habits of technological reason aren't the habits that foster spiritual insight, life wisdom, or transcendent meaning. So if technological reason is our default approach to life—if these are the habits that all our social institutions encourage us to adopt—then transcendent meaning will elude us.

Reflexive spiritualists think that literalism, scientism, rules and routine, and closure are cultural problems—not just religious problems. But they're keenly aware of the effect that these habits of thought have on religious life. They see technological reason as squeezing the transcendent out of life. But religion is supposed to help people connect with the transcendent—in fact, for reflexive spiritualists, this is the main point of religion, its truest purpose. So what happens when religion gets taken over by technological reason? In the next chapter, I describe reflexive spiritualists' sense of what happens to religion when we force it to fit the constraints of technological rationality.

4 FLAT RELIGION AND FLAKY SPIRITUALITY

I suppose it is tempting, if the only tool you have is a hammer, to treat
everything as if it were a nail.

—ABRAHAM MASLOW[1]

In the last chapter, I compared technical reason to a lens or filter
that we use to look at the world; this lens or filter makes some things
(literal facts, material objects, and procedural rules) easier to see,
and other things (the transcendent, the spiritual, deeper meanings)
harder to see. Another way to think of technical reason is like a fun-
house mirror that reflects reality back at us in a distorted way.
When people try to use this lens, filter, or mirror to look at the transcendent, they end up seeing weird, flattened, disfigured images.

For reflexive spiritualists, the transcendent is, by nature, too big
to be captured in technologically rational terms. But because technological rationality is so powerful in modern society, it has become
our default way of looking at everything, including the transcendent.
To use Maslow's imagery, it is as if technological rationality is the
only tool we have, and so we try to treat everything—including religion and spirituality—as if it were about material reality, concrete
fact, procedural rules, and conclusive answers.

So what does a technologically rational society do when confronted with talk about transcendence, spirituality, or God? It
does one of two things: (1) It tries to "rationalize" it—make it
fit into the terms of technological rationality and thereby squash
it into two dimensions. Or (2), it rejects it as totally irrational

and therefore illegitimate—untruthful, vacuous, and ridiculous. Reflexive spiritualists thought that modern society was continually misreading religion and spirituality in one or the other of these two ways, and was thereby making it even more difficult for people to find transcendent meaning. I'll address these two misreadings in turn.

Flat Religion: Rationalizing Transcendence

How do we make the larger-than-life transcendent fit into the box of technical reason? With literalism, scientism, and rules. These are dimensions of technological rationality, and they make sense to us, so we use them to try to make sense of the transcendent. So when people describe their spiritual experiences, we read them as literal descriptions of historical fact. When people offer their spiritual insights, we treat them as proto-scientific attempts to explain the natural world. When people talk about living in accord with the transcendent, we translate their words into ethical laws.

In American culture, these are familiar ways of thinking about religion. We often treat religion as if it were mostly about questions of historical fact: Did Adam and Eve really exist? What did Jesus's disciples really see after he was killed? Is it all just a bunch of lies? We also treat religion as an early attempt to answer scientific questions: How old is the earth? How did the universe as we know it come into existence? What caused human life? And we often treat religion as if it were all about right and wrong behaviors: What are we allowed to do, and what are we not allowed to do? We get into huge debates about which version of history, which answers, and which rules should be taught in schools or enforced by law.

The reflexive spiritualists I observed often used "not" statements to talk about these ways of understanding religion—for example, "God is *not* just a judge handing out rewards and punishments for specific behaviors" or "Genesis is *not* an argument about the truth or falsity of evolution." Usually, they would follow up with their own alternative ways of understanding God, or Genesis, or whatever dimension of religious life was on the table. Cecil, for example, often said that the fundamental message of Genesis is "behind this universe is God." "God underlies the universe" is a spiritual claim, not a scientific one. Cecil wasn't talking about the scientific origins of the universe, and he didn't think Genesis was talking about that, either. Cecil's implicit message is that once again, technical reason is just not a good enough way to relate to religion. It doesn't work—it doesn't allow us to get at transcendent meaning. If we insist on thinking of religion as in terms of history, science, and rules, then we're going to miss most of what religion has to offer. Instead, reflexive spiritualists say, we need to step outside those parameters and think about religion in different ways.

For example, First Church's Faith and Reason group spent one meeting discussing Karen Armstrong's book *The Battle for God*. The book resonated with group members' own opinions about how to interpret the Bible. In particular, they didn't like scriptural interpretations that focused on historical accuracy. This excerpt of their discussion begins with Bill, who had read the book and was leading the discussion about it:

BILL: She [Armstrong] says we have not been able to express the experience of the sacred in logical discursive terms, but instead have had recourse to mythology, which was never meant to describe history, but rather was an attempt to express internal events. Nonhistorical does not mean untrue. The dearth of myth has led us to having to discover psychoanalysis. Freud. She says reason represents the outermost rind of the mind. When I read that, I could see an orange, and you peel the rind.

ANGIE: The good stuff's all inside.

BILL: She says the fundamentalists have missed mythos as well; they have turned it into logos. Rational philosophy, that's when the literal reading of the Bible began.

HELEN: Genesis began this many years and days ago, this literalism.

BILL: The reaction to the theory of evolution has been, "We'll prove creation actually happened literally as it says." The bodily resurrection: resurrection doesn't have to mean the body is resuscitated. The trinity is a mythical expression, an attempt to describe the undescribable, not an attempt to prove God has three parts.

JESS: The logos-oriented tried to put it down as a formula, and that makes it unbelievable.

Bill, Angie, Helen, Jess, and the other members of the Faith and Reason group thought that it was a mistake to think about Biblical stories as nothing more than accurate or inaccurate descriptions of historical fact. In a literalistic world, "nonhistorical" means the same thing as "untrue," but reflexive spiritualists disagree with this assumption. Along with Armstrong, they reject the language of history and embrace the language of mythology as a better way of understanding the Bible. Mythology, they're saying, helps us get closer to the transcendent reality that the writers of the Bible were trying to convey, in a way that history just can't.

The Bible isn't about history; neither is it about science. For reflexive spiritualists, modern science doesn't cast doubt on scriptural stories, because the two aren't talking about the same things. Science is about finding causal explanations for natural events. By contrast, religious texts and other spiritual talk are about finding meaning in the natural world and responding to the natural world in ways that respect that meaning. For example, I attended a lecture called "Stardust, Telescopes, and God" that featured Chip Kobulnicky, an astronomer, and Richard Simon Hanson, a professor of religious studies. Chip and Simon both argued emphatically that religious stories are not attempts at scientific explanation, and that it's a mistake to see them that way.

SIMON: The Bible doesn't have attempts to explain things. The scientific way of thinking is recent, and it's very Western. This is why I sense no division between science and religion. This crazy idea that there is a big debate between science and religion is based on a poor understanding of both.

CHIP: The twentieth-century scientific viewpoint, and the Genesis-like viewpoint. The kinds of questions we ask are just not the same as the kinds of questions people asked three thousand years ago, and the kinds of answers we demand are different. So we have to be careful, are we asking the questions they were asking?

AUDIENCE MEMBER: Traditional stories are attempts to explain natural occurrences.

SIMON: No, they're not explaining them; they're responding to them. Noticing. I look, and I feel awe. I hear a cricket chirping, and I feel like joining it.

Again, the terms that technical reason offers us—the terms of science—just aren't up to the task of conveying transcendent meaning. Simon rejects the scientistic approach to the Bible and instead promotes a language of deep attention and responsiveness. For Simon and other reflexive spiritualists, when the Bible talks about nature, it's not trying to identify scientific causes and effects. Instead, it's trying to foster a spiritual relationship between people and nature. By insisting on seeing religious scriptures as proto-scientific explanations, we're missing out on the deeper meanings that those stories could convey.

Reflexive spiritualists also reject the idea that religion is mostly about ethical laws. As they see it, lists of right and wrong behaviors are the bottom-rung potential of an attempt to live in accord with the transcendent. If I want to live a life that's transcendently meaningful and spiritually truthful, then yes, it's true that I probably don't want to build my life around murder, theft, and lies. But that's hardly the essence of the spiritual life—if anything, it's one *outcome* of a spiritual life. At least, that's how reflexive spiritualists see it. But to actually live a transcendently meaningful life, we need a deeper foundation than that.

That deeper foundation, for reflexive spiritualists, is the fundamental spiritual connection that all people have with one another, with the natural world, and with spiritual reality—God or the transcendent. What matters is that people realize the fundamental interconnectedness of reality. Different religions express this insight in different ways: "we are one" or "we are brothers and sisters in Christ" or "we are all parts of one larger Body" or "all beings have Buddha-nature" or "there is only Brahman." When people experience themselves as fundamentally connected to everyone else, they find a much richer morality than they can find in lists of right and wrong.

Reflexive spiritualists' most benign interpretation of ethical laws is that they are behavioral guidelines created by people who themselves were experientially aware of the transcendent unity of creation. These spiritual leaders created ethical laws in an attempt to translate their insights into practical terms. They were trying to be helpful to people who didn't have that kind of fundamental sense of interrelatedness. So ethical laws are a kind of spiritual kindergarten—simplified translations of deeper insights. And the best thing about ethical laws is that they can remind people, in any morally tricky situation, to think about how they would behave if they were basing their behavior on, for example, faith in a brotherhood of man.

The folks at Common Ground were eloquent on this point. Jim, during a lecture on interdependence, told his students that behavioral laws are secondary to the more fundamental task of loving God:

> Jesus said, don't commit adultery, but also don't even think about adultery. Jesus was not just making it a stricter rule. That's too superficial an interpretation. He was saying, be less concerned with what you should do, because if your consciousness is loving, not clinging, that's more fundamental an issue. Saint Augustus said, "Love God and do what you will." If you love God, your actions will proceed from that, will be emanations of that love.

And Wayne, during a discussion of mysticism, said that moral rules are spiritually not as valuable—not as meaningful—as an innate compassion born of an experiential relationship with the divine:

The goal of the spiritual journey, what mystics become, they become exquisitely compassionate. Sensitive, they have a vast consciousness of the worth of it all. They're totally moral by nature. Pure love. Moral rules are a ladder; they're abstract and rational. If we become truly loving and compassionate, we don't need the rules. We don't need "morality." Mystics have a profound sense of connectedness with everyone and everything, and they realize that individual projects for happiness are illusory if they don't take into account the happiness of everyone and everything else.

Jim, Wayne, and other reflexive spiritualists rejected the idea that religion is mostly about rules. The "rules" approach to religion—like the scientistic approach and the "historical fact" approach—just isn't enough. It's just not that meaningful—not that helpful at connecting people with any kind of spiritual or transcendent reality. True compassion is closer to the truth and comes not from following rules but from cultivating spiritual experience.

When reflexive spiritualists look around them, they see people misinterpreting spirituality and religion by squeezing them into the terms of technological reason. In their eyes, relating to religion as if it were history, science, or law is mistaken and inadequate. That approach to religion misses the richness of the transcendent truth and replaces it with flattened-out, watered-down, formalized distortions. Instead, reflexive spiritualists speak of religions as mythologies that are revelatory of transcendent meaning. They speak of religiosity as deep attention and responsiveness to the divine and to the world. They speak of religious behavior as compassion born of an awareness of the transcendent unity of everyone and everything. It's a mistake, they're saying, to look to religious scriptures for lessons in history, science, and law. And it's equally a mistake to reject religion for not providing lessons in history, science, and law. Instead, they want us to look more deeply into religious scriptures to find what they're really about: insight, wisdom, and meaning.

Flaky Spirituality: The "Woo Woo" Factor

Reducing religion to history, science, and law may suck most of the meaning out of it, but at least it keeps it culturally legitimate. If religion is just about history, science, and law, then technological reason can make sense of it. But what about the spiritual, the transcendent, and the divine? We can't make sense of these ideas using technological reason. They don't fit into technological terms. And technological reason has become so powerful in modern society that we tend to judge everything by its standards. It's as if the only things that can count as real, legitimate, and valid are things that we can understand in terms of technological reason. And so technological reason dismisses this talk of transcendent meaning and spirituality, pronouncing it "irrational"—silly, flaky, and just plain nutty.

The people I observed were very aware of this prejudice. They sensed that their talk about transcendence and spirituality was being measured against a particular normative cultural standard. And that standard was this: Talk about the transcendent is embarrassing at best and dangerous at worst, and people who talk about transcendent meaning are flaky at best and delusional at worst. Reflexive spiritualists wondered just how far they could go with their talk about spiritual reality before being mocked and dismissed.

At First Church, people sometimes voiced this sense of risk when they talked about what it means to live a divinely inspired life. Pastor David put it in terms of how the people around Jesus responded to him:

> God, for Jesus, was an experiential reality. For that reason, we can say that he was a heathen. He seems to have had a spiritual presence around him much as has been described around the Dalai Lama. We can understand him as insane, as his family did, or as eccentric, or as dangerous, or a threat. Or we can understand him to have been filled with the spirit of God.

People sometimes misperceive spirituality, David is saying. They sometimes see it as insanity or eccentricity, and they find it threatening.

But for the most part, it was outside of religious institutions that people voiced the most concern about how spirituality gets perceived. This makes sense: in Chapter 2, I talked about how modern society has differentiated—divided into separate institutions to deal with separate concerns. We've designated churches, synagogues, and other formal religious organizations as the proper places for any kind of talk about spirituality and the transcendent. Outside these institutions, spiritual talk becomes more suspect.

Writer Gregg Levoy leads workshops for people about following callings in their work and in their lives—for example, if they feel a calling to become a singer or artist, or to take up a political cause, or to start a business or nonprofit organization, or to uproot and move to another country, or to devote their lives to charitable work. These workshops aren't associated with any religious tradition—they're part of the broader spiritual culture. During one workshop, Gregg asked participants to write down what they thought other people would say if they decided to follow their calling; he then asked them to share what they had written down. Here are some of the answers participants gave:

- "You're crazy. You're making more money than all your cousins, you're the winner—Aren't you happy?"
- "I always knew there was something flaky about her."
- "I always thought you were crazy."
- "That's too woo woo for business."
- "Do we have to tell anyone?"
- "What am I supposed to tell my mother?"

Then Gregg chimed in with his own:

> "Where did you come up with the notion of God, coming from the family you came from?" That was my mom's response to the *Callings* book. She was astonished that I had a spiritual life. I heard it as, a spiritual life is so anti-intellectual, so intellectually creepy, so intellectually tacky.

As these people well knew, in a society that's all about being "rational," a spiritual calling is not a legitimate basis for action. We are supposed to use logic and practical reason to make our decisions. To instead follow an intuited "calling" is to risk your status as a reasonable, responsible, sane person.

Common Grounders had the same sense of being on the margins of legitimacy. Ron encouraged Common Ground students to turn to each other for community and support in the face of cultural disapproval:

> Our culture doesn't support what we do. We all know a lot of people who absolutely think we're crazy for doing what we're doing here today. We don't have a society that gives us strong support for this, so we need spiritual friends.

In the spirituality-at-work movement, the talk went beyond "crazy" and "flaky" to "dangerous." During a discussion led by consultant Jack Shea, participants talked about how risky it felt to mention spirituality in their workplaces:

BRIAN: The largest challenge is I feel like a stranger in a strange land. I talk about doing spiritually centered work, but I speak about it in a different way because most people aren't prepared to hear it that way, but even then I still see a fear. People fear that; they don't know what it would mean to bring that into work.

LARRY: I get these flyers for seminars about spirituality and work, and I think, "Oh my God! Should I circulate this, or should I *burn* it?" There's an "Oh my God!" to it.

The biggest obstacle to talking about the transcendent was what I call the Woo Woo factor. Reflexive spiritualists—especially those talking outside of churches and other religious institutions—believed that other people thought that spiritual talk was flaky, tacky, wacky, and "out there." In the contemporary United States, the New Age movement carries the burden of the Woo Woo factor. Any kind of spirituality that people don't immediately recognize as belonging to a longstanding world religion gets called "New Agey," which also, apparently, means "okay to make fun of." So Common Grounders, for example, took pains to distinguish themselves from the New Age movement. They characterized the New Age movement as shallow and lax, lacking in depth, rigor, and commited engagement with the traditions it borrows. In a workshop about the soul, for example, Jim made a point of saying,

> Soul work is not stop and smell the roses. It's not lightweight, New Age, everything is beautiful. It involves wrestling with difficult and dark things. Soul work is embracing the fullness of the creation. It includes death work, pain work, committing to look at things you might rather ignore.

Jim was encouraging his students to engage in "soul work," and part of his argument was that it requires serious attention to complex and difficult things, and therefore, it's not flaky.[2]

The Woo Woo factor also made it hard for reflexive spiritualists to explain their spirituality to other people. During a Common Ground social hour, two women complained to me that they had a hard time describing Common Ground to their friends. One of them put it this way:

> When I tell people about Common Ground, they think it's all froo froo and crystals. So I tell them how smart people are, how well-educated the people are, the teachers are people with PhDs, it's like a lecture. We should talk about this in Common Ground—how to explain Common Ground without sounding froo froo.

This woman didn't want her friends to dismiss Common Ground as shallow and irrational—"froo froo and crystals." Her solution was to emphasize the things about Common Ground that conform to rational standards: the teachers' credentials and the educational tone.

Sociologist Courtney Bender observed this same fear of flakiness in her study of the spirituality movement in Cambridge, Massachusetts. She noticed that when the people she interviewed told her about their spiritual experiences, they would "deflect alternative explanations that might mark [them] as momentarily insane, daydreaming, or stimulated by some forgotten or unknown subconscious suggestion."[3] She noticed, too, that they sometimes seemed to be trying to convince her of the validity of religious experience in general. Bender interpreted this kind of defensiveness as an attempt to draw her as a social scientist into their experience and so to gain scientific validation—or at least an objective hearing—for their experiences.[4] It seems equally likely that they saw her as a representative of technological rationality and were fighting some of the same rationalistic prejudices that the people I studied were so aware of. Social scientists are notorious for insisting on reductive explanations of religious experience—arguing that religious experience must really be about something else, such as class inequality (Karl Marx), the power of society (Emile Durkheim), or unresolved childhood crises (Sigmund Freud). But Bender's status as a social scientist might not even have come into play—her interviewees might simply have been aware, as the people I observed were, that we live in a technologically rational society and that technological rationality just doesn't have any non-reductive way to understand spiritual experience and so has no choice but to either find some "rational" explanation for it or else dismiss it as flakiness and insanity.

In my own research, I heard many examples of reflexive spiritualists' fear of flakiness, but the best one took place among businesspeople at Gregg Levoy's *Callings* workshop. When Gregg asked participants how others might react if they followed their calling, Ruth had said, "They'd say, 'That's too woo woo for business.'" Later on that day, Gregg asked participants to write down the payoffs they might expect if they chose to follow their calling, and he again asked volunteers to share what they had written. Ruth again raised her hand:

RUTH: I surprised myself: I wrote the word "transcendence" as a benefit— becoming something larger, or connecting with something larger. It surprised me that I wrote that.

GREGG: Because it's too woo woo for business?

RUTH: No, I just never thought of myself as transcendent.

PATTY: Most business is full of woo woo; they don't realize it—they're pretending. Full of—

JASON: Shit.

PATTY: Thank you.

GREGG: Oh! I took "woo woo" to mean spiritual things.

LYNN: Yeah—business will put up with crap but not woo woo.

RICHARD: So it's the dilemma of woo woo versus doo doo.

"Woo woo versus doo doo." With these words, Richard perfectly voices the dilemma that reflexive spiritualists believe they face. On one hand, when they look out at modern society, they see it as preoccupied with the basest functions of humanity; they see it as a wasteland. On the other hand, they fear that their efforts to introduce some sense of larger meaning and purpose into that society would be dismissed as "woo woo"—too weird, too flaky, inappropriate, irrational, and invalid.

In part, this is a dilemma of language. If something has to be "rational" to be taken seriously and seen as legitimate, then how do you describe something that *transcends* rationality? How do you talk about something that isn't just rational, but also isn't just irrational? The folks at Common Ground attempted to solve this problem by invoking the language of transcendence itself: they described the transcendent as neither rational nor irrational, but "transrational." Ron brought up the idea of transrationality one day when he was talking about the ineffability of God:

> Ineffability means that it can't be expressed. Like the first line of the *Tao Te Ching*: "The Tao that can be spoken is not the eternal Tao." The god that can be contained in rational language is not God. This is why Tillich points us to "the God beyond God"—language just can't contain it, because it's transrational. I don't mean irrational—transrational. There are three levels: the prerational, the rational, and the transrational. The rational is very important—as a college teacher, most of our task is getting students from the prerational level, where they just have opinions, to the rational. But in our culture, we stop there. We stop with the rational. Other cultures affirm the third step, the level of the transrational, the things that can't be understood in rational language. Our culture doesn't affirm that.[5]

Ron is introducing new vocabulary to his students, and our words form our categories of thought. As the philosopher Ludwig Wittgenstein once wrote, "The limits of my language are the limits of my world." And as many sociologists have argued, our shared vocabulary is what makes things culturally possible, culturally real. If we don't have the words to talk about an idea, then that idea remains culturally invisible, culturally illegitimate.[6] So when Ron introduces words like "prerationality" and "transrationality," he's offering his students—and the culture more broadly—a more refined way of thinking about the nonrational. He's saying that the world doesn't just fit into "rational" and "irrational"—that there's more to it than that. And that the idea of a spiritual or transcendent reality, the idea of God, isn't necessarily *irrational* just because it's *nonrational*. He's saying that rationality is not, in fact, the pinnacle of our ability to discern truth—that there are ways of knowing that encompass and go beyond rationality. And that these other ways of knowing—these transrational ways of knowing—are what allow us to be aware of transcendent reality and to find transcendent meaning.

5 USING REASON TO FIND MEANING IN RELIGION AND LIFE

Reason is not the enemy of meaning. Technical reason, our antagonist in chapters 3 and 4, is not the only kind of reason we have inherited from the Enlightenment. Another kind of reason—intellectual reason—is one of our greatest resources in the pursuit of meaning. Intellectual reason is what we call our ability to consider ideas deliberately, to draw conclusions, and to raise new questions. It's these abilities that allow us to look thoughtfully into religious traditions and find deeper meanings in them. Intellectual reason makes thoughtful religious inquiry possible: it enables us to reflect on religious traditions, texts, languages, practices, and images and ask what they might mean.[1]

Intellectual rationality is a modern tradition. We've built colleges and universities around it, we teach students to use it systematically, and we've developed academic disciplines to harness its use to create new knowledge, new ideas, and new meanings. Reflexive spiritualists draw on these intellectual traditions for tools that they can use to make religion more meaningful. This is the heart of reflexive spirituality: the *way of being religious* that it fosters. Reflexive spiritualists use intellectual tools to bring more meaning to religious stories, traditions, and symbols—to make religion come alive for modern minds.

This chapter describes four tools that reflexive spiritualists use to make religion meaningful: the reflexivity for which reflexive spirituality is named, metaphor, pluralism, and mysticism. With each of these tools, reflexive spiritualists draw from the tradition of intellectual reason to point to meanings that transcend the limits of reason. Each tool helps make religion *possible* for educated seekers by making it *meaningful* to them.

Reflexivity: Religion Is About Questions, Not Answers

Many educated seekers are turned off by dogmatism—claims of one right way, one set of correct beliefs, and one authoritative and incontrovertible truth. Educated seekers aren't interested in religions that offer definitive answers. Instead, they find meaning in questions. They trust ongoing inquiry more than hard-and-fast answers to life's deepest questions. The concept of reflexivity captures this idea of a commitment to ongoing spiritual inquiry. When I am being reflexive, I'm mentally stepping back from my own perspective and recognizing that there are many other perspectives that may each be valuable and worthwhile and that might inform and enrich my own perspective.

Reflexivity is about the use of reason. When we are reflexive, we're engaging our minds to question assumptions, consider possibilities, and evaluate alternatives. Like the practice of systematic doubt in modern science, a commitment to reflexivity means recognizing that while we do find answers to our questions, our answers are always provisional. Sociologist Anthony Giddens put it this way: "Modernity . . . insists that all knowledge takes the form of hypotheses: claims which may very well be true, but which are in principle always open to revision and may have at some point to be abandoned."[2] With reflexive spirituality, we apply this practice of systematic doubt to our own religious worldview by making a habit of reflecting on our religious ideas in light of other alternatives.

In place of certainty, reflexivity offers possibility. Truth is ever-evolving, and the potential for meaning is endless. Reflexivity is creative; it asks for openness and honesty: What does this scripture passage really say to me? What was the writer trying to say? What do I think about this argument? What do you think about it? What does this story crystallize, illuminate, conceal? What deeper truths do these words or this practice or that imagery evoke? How can I integrate these deeper meanings into my approach to life? Reflexivity is thoughtful and imaginative; it invites complexity, subtlety, multiplicity, sensitivity, and nuance.

Journalist Winifred Gallagher captured this idea of spiritual inquiry in the title of one of her books: *Working on God*. In a public radio interview, she said:

> I called the book *Working on God* because I really think what's happening religiously in this country is a shift . . . from religion as dispensing answers to religion as being a process of pursuing questions. So when I go to church on Sunday, I don't go for received truths; I go to work on God, and I feel the more I do that, the more questions I have, but they're different questions that are taking me further into a very profound inquiry.

"Working on God" was exactly the attitude that David and other leaders promoted at First United Methodist Church. In a sermon he called "Wrestling with God," David told the Biblical story of Jacob and pointed out that in the story, God renames Jacob "Israel," which means "one who wrestles with God." David wrote this sermon for graduating high school seniors who would be heading off to college in the fall. After telling the story of Jacob, David spoke to the graduates about the spiritual questioning that his own college years inspired:

> I grew up in a Christian family that was involved in the church. I never missed a Sunday service or Sunday School. I was part of that culture that assumed that Christianity had all the answers and I didn't need to question them. Then I went to college, where I met people of other religions and people with no religion who seemed perfectly content to have no religion, and I had professors who said that no thinking person could believe the tenets of Christianity.
>
> Leaving home is the experience of everything you took for granted is called into question. You read Freud, who said that religion is an illusion, a crutch used by the emotionally weak. Or Marx, who called religion the opiate of the masses.
>
> One way to deal with that is to put your fingers in your ears, blinders on your eyes, and to refuse to deal with it. Ignore it. Say, "I've never dealt with that before; I'm not gonna deal with it now."
>
> The story of Jacob tells us that leaving home is part of growing in faith. We are to worship the Lord our God with all our heart, with all our soul, and with all our *mind*. God gives us our mind, and we need to engage it.

In another sermon, a sermon about Jesus given as Easter approached, David encouraged his congregation to take religious authority lightly—to replace unquestioning acceptance with thoughtful engagement and personal honesty:

> I can tell you who Jesus is for me, what he means to me. For me, Jesus is the one who, for me, leads me to my best understanding of God . . . and is the model of authentic living. But you can't say, "David thinks this about Jesus, so that's right," and think no more about it. You must for yourself decide who this man is for you. Each of you must ask yourself, Who is he to you?
>
> Jesus asked his disciples, "What do they say about me, who I am?" And they told him, some say John the Baptist, others say Elijah, and others Jeremiah or one of the prophets. Then he asked them, "But who do *you* say that I am?"
>
> That is the religious question for Christians or people who want to be Christians. You can listen to others, read others, talk with others, but you must ask it of yourself and decide yourself. To do this, you must immerse yourself in the Bible, other texts, authors like Marcus Borg, other ideas, and converse, converse with each other because that's how we learn and think about it—we're a social animal, and we need to engage with each other. But in the end, we each must answer for ourselves.

Common Ground teachers promoted this same sense of personal responsibility. For example, during one class, Ron encouraged his students to cultivate authority over their own spiritual development:

> A lot of us did suffer from a kind of lock-step spirituality that I think was very harmful. . . . Each person needs to look at theirself and ask, "What's my next step?" . . . I'm not saying that opposed to a dictatorship is a happy-go-lucky approach. I believe in a discernment of appropriateness at a particular time.

Ron's students also preferred thoughtful interrogation to quick answers. During a class break, one student engaged her friend in a conversation about religious identity, saying, "I don't know what I am—universalist?" Her friend replied, "There doesn't have to be an answer; it's the process of trying to figure it out that's important."

In these examples, people are being reflexive (or encouraging others to be reflexive) about *themselves*—to question, consider, and be open to revising their own spiritual outlook in light of other possibilities. But for members of religious traditions, spiritual reflexivity is not just a personal practice—it's also a community practice. If I am a Christian, for example, and I and others in my congregation are actively questioning, considering, and revising our spiritual views, then we are also necessarily questioning, considering, and revising Christianity. For reflexive spiritualists, this is what makes the difference between a living tradition and dead traditionalism. Reinterpretation and revision don't threaten religious traditions, but invigorate them, renew them—give them new life. During a call-in radio show with spiritual author Elizabeth Lesser, a caller named Judy compared this process to the new growth of a tree:

> One of the things that is said in the Baha'i teachings is that religion is like a tree, and it grows and it comes to fruition, and then it's sort of a time of a new tree having to come and grow to fruition, and that religion is a constant renewing, like spiritual springtime, and we have to recognize that all of these many beautiful traditions are just part of that tree.

At First Church, this reflexive renewal focused on Christian tradition. Members had the sense that United Methodism specifically, and official Christianity generally, should be open to criticism from lay Christians. The Theology for the Twenty-First Century adult education class embraced this attitude by spending four months discussing Episcopal Bishop John Shelby Spong's book *Why the Church Must Change or Die*. First Church members' insistence on the revisability of Christian tradition often took the form of criticisms of "the church," as when a member of the class said, "The church doesn't really want you to think. Questions and comments are automatically put down as 'You don't do this kind of thing in the Methodist church.'" During a discussion of the gospel of John in the Reading the Bible Intelligently class, participants criticized the church for failing to talk about spiritual healing:

MARTHA: I think the healing stories, especially the story about the son of the official, is about the health-giving power of the gospels. That faith can heal, that wholeness of mind, body, and spirit does matter in healing.
CECIL: The churches have really not emphasized this enough, have not dealt with this, and Christian Science arose in America as a response to this lack.

More strongly, reflexivity toward Christian tradition sometimes meant actively rejecting official interpretations of traditional symbols. In a sermon about the crucifixion of Jesus, for example, David explained the church's traditional interpretation as one of sacrifice, in which God required restitution for human sin, and Jesus's death provided that restitution. After giving this explanation, David paused, and then said this:

> This image of God sending a son to endure as a sacrifice this kind of crucifixion, I find totally unsatisfactory. To put it more strongly, *I don't believe it for a minute.* That the only way God can forgive us is to have someone endure this kind of inhuman suffering, I find totally beyond belief. But I do believe that the cross is at the heart of the faith. So I want to tell you about the images that nourish my soul, what the cross means to me.

David was an ordained and experienced Christian minister and the leader of a large congregation. He gave this sermon about the central Christian symbol to a full house on a Sunday shortly before Easter. He said, in effect, "I can tell you this symbol's official interpretation. I can also tell you that I totally reject that interpretation. But I don't at all reject the symbol, and here is why." Christianity, for David, must be a reflexive tradition. It must be open to reinterpretation if it is to remain spiritually vital.[3]

The teachers at Common Ground shared his insistence. Ron, for example, invited his students to reinterpret the practice of Shabbat, or Sabbath, in accord with their sense of its truest purpose:

RON: The purpose of Shabbat is to recognize the importance of rest and renewal by setting aside a day for reflection and renewal. How can we take this notion even more adaptably into our lives? What about Sabbath as a principle, or rhythm that could be brought into the day or the week in different ways for different people? For example, the morning. Some period of the morning could be your space for inspirational reading, for prayer, for meditative music, or to walk in nature. Any way in which one punctuates this hectic world with periods of silence and rest. One can be creative about the rhythm of Shabbat.

MICHAEL: I'm suspicious of creative interpretations of Shabbat. It raises the old question of are there rules, or do we make the rules? It's calming to me to check my stock positions—but that's a ridiculous interpretation of

Shabbat. It's worthwhile to be suspicious of creativity; it may be that your creativity is being used to subvert Shabbat.

RON: Yeah, but on the other side, you get the problem of observing the rules but violating the spirit, the purpose of Shabbat. For example, leaving your TV on for twenty-six hours so you're not technically violating the rule about touching tools. So the point is to work through it yourself and recognize everyone's Shabbat will be different. But to focus first on the purpose of Shabbat. Yeah, it's important to have a community to reinforce it and to keep you honest, but.

Just as David embraced the core religious symbol of the cross, Ron embraced the idea and practice of Shabbat. But like David, Ron wanted to open that symbol up to a wider array of interpretations than the ones that are most familiar or most acceptable to religious authorities. Ron's spiritual life was not nourished by a technological interpretation of Shabbat as a set of rules about allowable behavior on a particular day of the week. The letter of the law, for Ron, was not enough. Instead, he sought the symbol's wisdom.

Learning, Reflexivity, and Religious Studies

Learning is part and parcel of reflexivity. The reflexive spiritualists I observed sought out teachers, experts, and authors who could feed their desire for thoughtful spiritual ideas to play with and learn from. Sometimes, this search led them to scholars in the field of religious studies, including the psychological work of William James and Carl Jung, the historical work of Mircea Eliade, Karen Armstrong, Marcus Borg, and John Dominick Crossan, the sociological work of Peter Berger, the mythological studies of Joseph Campbell, the philosophical work of Huston Smith and Ken Wilber, and the anthropological work of John Neihardt. Beyond these specific scholars, the discipline of religious studies in general seemed to me to be an important institutional support for spiritual reflexivity. Like reflexive spirituality, the discipline of religious studies simultaneously promotes a concern with religious frames of reference and a commitment to rational inquiry. The entire ethos of religious studies encourages the kind of reflexive approach to religious tradition that I saw in my field sites.[4]

This "religious studies ethos" was especially apparent at Common Ground, where both Ron and Jim had graduate training in religious studies. For example, Ron once taught a class about historian Thomas Cahill's book *The Gift of the Jews.* Here, he's discussing the biblical story of Abraham and Isaac in terms of the image of God that this story offers:

> This story highlights how different this god is from prior, predictable gods. This is a god of surprises. This god is not controllable, this god cannot be manipulated by sacrifices or ritual. This god is the initiator. He is beyond human reasoning. Anything and everything is possible. Faith now has a place it never had before; the future is more open than in cyclical religion. . . .
>
> The part of the Bible where God says, what is usually translated as "I am that I am," is better translated as "I will be as I will be." This is where *Yahweh* comes from. In Hebrew, it's written YHWH, no vowels. It's very cryptic, called the "unpronounceable name." But it's very consistent with Abraham's story: an unnamable, mysterious, willful, unimagable god, who breaks the mold of gods.
>
> If I had to summarize the Old Testament god in one word, it would be "with." It's always "I'll be with you." In the Old Testament, the divine is revealed as the great "with" of human experience. The Old Testament emphasizes God's continual presence in the creation.

Here, Ron is emphasizing religious reflexivity not just in what he's saying, but also in his entire style of analysis. "God," here, is not a closed symbol with just one meaning. There is no possibility of a "correct" image of God; "God" as a category is wholly constructed. But its transcendent referent—that mysterious reality that the word "god" is meant to point to—is considered really important. The God of the Hebrew tradition is "this god"—one instance, one example, one moment, of the larger category of all possible gods, which themselves are crystallizations of the more abstract concept of "the divine."

Ron's exegesis of the Hebrew Bible's image of God is not an appeal to a totally authoritative tradition that offers certainty about the nature of God. And it isn't a critical analysis aimed at translating the tradition into secular categories of thought. What it is is an attempt to line up one more image of the divine, in an ongoing effort to make the idea of God meaningful. Ron is offering an answer, not to the question "What is God really like?" nor to the question "What real facts is all this god-talk disguising?" but rather to the question "What might this word 'God' mean?" Another day, another Biblical story, or another religious tradition, will be mined for the image of the divine that it offers, and this image will be placed alongside the Abrahamic image as another possible answer. So the symbol itself—the word "god"—is ever-evolving. Its meaning is only limited by the reflexive capacity of the people who engage with the tradition.

At First Church, David used religious history in a similar way—he drew especially on Marcus Borg's and John Dominick Crossan's work on the historical Jesus to help members draw new meanings out of traditional Christian stories. And in the secular field sites I studied, several lecturers and radio interviewees either were scholars in religious studies themselves or drew on these scholars' writings in their own work.

Reflexive spiritualists aren't only or even mostly interested in scholarly ideas about religion, but they are interested in these ideas when they seem to offer food for the spiritual quest. More broadly, religious studies seems to provide a space where religious traditions can meet rational inquiry on a somewhat level playing field, and that's exactly what a reflexive spirituality requires.

"We're the Meaning-Makers": Embracing the Responsibility of Reflexivity

Religious reflexivity is nothing new. Theologians, bishops, and other religious elites have practiced it for centuries as they sought to make their religions meaningful for new generations in new contexts.[5] But the spirit of democracy runs deep in the United States, and now, ordinary people are taking reflexivity into their own hands. Helen, at a meeting of First Church's Faith and Reason group, put this meaning-making democracy into words during a discussion of the origins of the universe. The group had been talking about the theory of the Big Bang when Tim asked, "What does this have to do with religion?" Helen jumped in:

> *Vastness*, we're so small and insignificant, yet at the same time, here we are, all dinky, coming to an understanding of this. We're tiny, and we're *it. We're the meaning-makers*. The guy on *this* side of the telescope gives meaning.

This spiritual authority is a rush—when we're the meaning-makers, then the possibilities for meaning are suddenly as limitless as our imaginations. This spiritual authority is also a responsibility—when we're the meaning-makers, we can't sit back and let others dictate truth.

Helen and other reflexive spiritualists actively took on responsibility for renewing religious tradition, or as they often put it, for "making the religion speak to us." So at First Church one day, Carl spoke to the Faith and Reason group about his interest in the historical work of the Jesus Seminar, whose

members have argued that much of the Christian New Testament is historically inaccurate:

> Some people say to me, if you believe what they say, then you're an
> atheist, that's the end of being Christian for you. I don't accept that at
> all. What I see us doing is, we're trying to get at a Christianity that
> speaks to us in terms of our everyday experience and accumulated
> knowledge. I think it will make for a stronger theology.

Cecil, too, saw reflexivity as a Christian responsibility. During their discussions of Bishop Spong's *Why the Church Must Change or Die*, members of
the Theology for the Twenty-First Century class considered what Spong's
criticisms might mean for Christian education. Cecil felt that such criticisms
and questions were a necessary part of responsible teaching:

> Young people, college students, find religion irrelevant, and our chal-
> lenge is to state the gospel in terms that engage them where they live.
> Spong is engaged in that effort. He goes for a restatement of beliefs
> that the postmodern mind, or what he calls the modern scientific
> mind, can buy into, accept, and live with with integrity.
>
> When I was raising children, I felt often that I was having to un-
> teach my children what they were taught in Sunday School. I think
> this class is, we're inviting ourselves and each other to read things that
> challenge our ideas. I hope it's an invitation to others to talk about
> the things we believe, to explore what we really mean and believe, and
> I hope that it's not that we all get together and say we're superior
> to those slobs who haven't considered these questions. . . . We're not
> here to say the traditional language is wrong and people who like it
> shouldn't. If it do ring true, blessed are you, but if it don't, for those of
> us for whom that language doesn't ring true, we need a way to deal
> with that.

Common Ground teachers also saw reflexivity as a spiritual responsibility—
their goal wasn't to simply "pick and choose" what they liked from religious
traditions, but to actively contribute to those traditions by making them meaningful for modern ears. In describing the work of religious historian Marcus
Borg, for example, Ron told a class that Borg's books are about "how Christians
can be Christian in a postmodern age." He described the work of Rabbi Rami
Shapiro similarly:

In *Minyan*, Shapiro said, "I wanted something more" than what he was getting from his religious education. This is common for a lot of people. Some give it up, give up their religion. Some live in a dualistic world where the temple or church represents a sort of fairy-tale world where you talk about spirits and miracles that seem absurd in the outside world. Others have to find some integrity, have to find how it fits together. How to be Jewish or Christian in a way that's consonant with the world we live in.

"To make a stronger theology." "To restate beliefs for the postmodern mind." "To create a Christianity for a postmodern age." "To find some integrity." This is the big responsibility of reflexivity: participation. To not keep questions, criticisms, and challenges to ourselves, but to voice them in the ongoing conversation that makes religious traditions come alive.

The spiritual democracy of reflexivity brings with it a second responsibility: to accept disagreement and ambiguity. At First Church, Cecil periodically repeated the old joke, "Wherever two United Methodists are gathered, you have three opinions." At one point during the Theology for the Twenty-First Century class, a participant commented facetiously, "I look forward to the end of this class when we decide what the minimum requirements are to be a Christian!" Cecil responded, "Apparently, agreeing with one another is not one of the requirements! We need to recognize that Christians will disagree, and we must find fellowship despite that. We must love each other and be in fellowship even though we don't agree." David echoed this sentiment from the pulpit:

> If you believe as I do that the Bible was not dictated by God but is the work of especially sensitive people trying to put down their experience of God, trying to describe the experience of God in their people, the breath of spirit and the influence of spirit as they have experienced it . . . you see that the Bible is a history of disagreements, and stops and starts, and without those disagreements and stops and starts, we'd still be in the days of an eye for an eye and a tooth for a tooth, and we would take adulterous women and stone them to death.

Common Ground teachers also found wisdom in accepting disagreement and uncertainty. A teacher named Ron Kidd, for example, ended his class about Socrates with this message:

Socrates says his wisdom is the wisdom to know that he is not wise where he is not, versus thinking he's wise. He's the only one who'll admit that he doesn't know what is good and true and beautiful and right and just. His is the wisdom of realizing that he does not know anything. In that not-knowing, he's able to pursue the search for wisdom. The wisest course is to begin by acknowledging your own ignorance, begin by not knowing. Zen Buddhists call this "don't-know mind."

Reflexivity offers freedom—a release from the dictates of dogma. But as a spiritual practice, its meaning is much deeper than a simple rejection of ecclesiastical authority. Reflexive spiritualists encourage one another to think critically about religious tradition, engage thoughtfully with the ideas of others, contribute to a collective conversation, and accept uncertainty. For all this, what reflexive spiritualists gain is *possibility*—the possibility of new meaning in old traditions.[6]

Metaphor: Religion Is About Truth, Not Fact

Reflexive spiritualists love metaphor. Unlike literal language, metaphor has the power to evoke the *ineffable*—that which can't be expressed literally. The language of fact and precision is inadequate to capture life's deepest meanings, largest truths, and most profound experiences. That's why our best representations of love, loss, death, joy, and hope lie not in scientific journals and news reports, but in poetry, film, art, literature, and song.

In Chapter 3, I spoke of modern society's love affair with literalism and described the ways that literal thinking limits our ability to find meaning in life and religion. Literalism insists that religion's truth lies in its facticity, and that for a religious story to be true, it must be factual. From this point of view, to interpret a religious story metaphorically is to weaken it, to drain it of truthfulness. But "That's just a metaphor" is not a sentence that a reflexive spiritualist would ever say. In reflexive spirituality, there's nothing "just" about metaphors. On the contrary, for reflexive spiritualists, metaphorical interpretation is the very best possible approach to religious imagery. Spiritual life is by nature subtle, profound—transcendent. Spiritual truth is just too big to be captured by words that can only ever mean one thing.[7]

But metaphor, rich metaphor, invites the imagination and allows an infinite flow of new meanings over time. With metaphor, an image, word, or story can mean something new in every new context. Consider the book you read when you were ten years old, that meant something different to you then than it did when you read it again years later. Consider the song on the radio that you never paid much attention to, until one day something changed in your life and that song took on new meaning. Consider the movie that your family sees one way and your friends see a different way. So too with religious language and ritual: when it's taken metaphorically, it can keep on giving meaning. As the philosopher Paul Ricoeur has said, every metaphor contains a "surplus of meaning."[8]

Many scholars believe that metaphor is a modern concept—that premodern speakers frequently used what we now call metaphor, but didn't distinguish it from other kinds of truth.[9] But in the modern world, we have elevated literal, factual, testable truth to such importance that we have come to see it as different from other kinds of truth, including metaphorical truth. There is a benefit to distinguishing metaphorical truth from literal truth: if we make this distinction, then each kind of truth gets to develop according to its own logic. Science and history have specialized in literal truth and can tell us more observable facts than we've ever known. Likewise, by approaching religious texts and practices metaphorically, we are able not only to respect and incorporate the literal truths that science and history offer, but also to create a wealth of transcendent meanings beyond what science and history can offer. As Simon said in the last chapter, the idea that science and religion must conflict is based on a poor understanding of both.

For many reflexive spiritualists, metaphor has saved religion. Through metaphorical interpretation, religious scriptures and rituals that had been empty and opaque have now become meaningful. So for example, during a discussion of exile, Cecil asked the Theology for the Twenty-First Century class if they ever felt "in exile in the faith." Reggie answered, "I was in exile, for twenty years. This—David, you, us—is what brought me back—a nonliteralist approach."

Pastor David cultivated this nonliteralist approach to meaning during his sermons. In a sermon about the Apostles' and Nicene Creeds, he used metaphor to draw meaning out of the story of the virgin birth of Jesus:

> The Gospels are not a literal history. They are an interpretation of the meaning of Jesus for the gospel-writers. They were written for religious instruction, not for historical description. . . .
>
> For example, the virgin birth. The virgin birth is mentioned in two gospels, not in the other two, and nowhere in the writings of Paul. We can't say that historically, literally, Jesus was born of a virgin—we don't have the tools to prove that. We do know that Jesus was not the only

one of his day who was described as "born of a virgin." "He was born of a virgin" was the language used in the time to say, "In this person, we have an extraordinary event that can't be explained in ordinary human terms."

Does the story of the virgin birth have any meaning? Is it true? For David, the answers to these questions lie not in assertions of factual accuracy or inaccuracy, but rather in the story's capacity to point to the extraordinary and ineffable. Literalistic approaches to scriptures miss this dimension of truth—something David alluded to in a later sermon about the crucifixion:

> There's no question about the historicity of the crucifixion. The story of the crucifixion appears in the gospels, which are not unbiased, and it also appears in secular writings. There is no historical question about the historical reality of the part of the creed that says, "Jesus suffered under Pontius Pilate, was crucified, died, and was buried." But what is the message of the crucifixion? How can we interpret it? What does it say to us? How can the story of the crucifixion nourish our spiritual lives?

History doesn't offer obvious meaning, David was telling his flock; meaning requires that we go beyond history into interpretation. A member of David's congregation expressed this same preference for meaning over fact at a meeting of the Reading the Bible Intelligently class:

> The purpose of good fiction—good fiction, *War and Peace, Gone with the Wind,* not supermarket-checkout fiction—is to tell the truth. *War and Peace* reveals truths about human nature. I can go ahead and call the Bible fiction, but the purpose of fiction is to tell the truth, and the Bible has great insight into truth, and I can understand it better that way.

Ron, at Common Ground, voiced the logic of this preference for metaphor: only through metaphor can we approach the core of religion: the transcendence that literal language is so inadequate to convey. During a discussion of Christian eschatology, Ron said:

> One reinterpretation of the last judgment is an ongoingness of life, of whatever kind. . . . That's the first judgment, the judgment of the individual life. The second judgment, of the end of the world—the same thing, an ongoingness in some other form. Not a continuing human

calendar. Not bound by our ideas of time and space. So, what we have here are two mysteries that can't be pinned down in our temporal and spatial language. . . .

I'm really afraid of too much speculation about before and after life. . . . I believe and intuit the ongoingness of life, and I derive some meaning from the different metaphors that are used, but for me, they're fingers pointing at the moon; they point to a mystery that transcends what we can understand. Life comes from God, and life returns to God. What's the exact nature of that? I don't know.

Like a curve approaching an asymptote, our language reaches for transcendent truth but never quite touches it. Or in the Buddhist image that Ron uses, religious language is like a finger pointing to the moon: to truly see the moon, we need to focus not on the finger, but beyond it, in the direction it points.[10]

The Role of History: Recovering Lost Metaphors

The philosopher Paul Ricoeur once wrote, "modern man . . . alone can recognize the myth as myth, because he alone has reached the point where history and myth become separate."[11] The other side of Ricoeur's observation is that modern people alone can recognize history as history, without confusing it with myth.

Reflexive spiritualists love metaphor, but they also value scientific history. What's important, they insist, is to distinguish between the two. It's a mistake, they say, to interpret the Christian Bible as an inerrant record of historical fact. Instead, they call on history to help seekers understand the context in which the Bible was written. They want to understand this context because they recognize that metaphors mean different things in different communities, times, and places, and they want to understand what Biblical stories might have meant for their original communities.

What were the writers of the Bible trying to say? What did the language they used mean to their audiences? Reflexive spiritualists seek out information about Biblical times to help answer these questions. Through this kind of historical work, reflexive spiritualists hope to uncover meanings that might not occur to a modern audience and so to gain even more meaning from religious texts. As a member of First Church's Theology for the Twenty-First Century class said, "We don't understand symbols. We don't understand what the language would have meant to them. We've lost that. We need to get that back."

To "get that back," reflexive spiritualists turn to scholars: religious historians, linguists, and ministers with training in these areas. Some members of First Church, for example, were attracted to the work of the Jesus Seminar, a group of religious historians who meet regularly to discuss and vote on the historical accuracy of the words and actions attributed to Jesus in the New Testament as well as other aspects of early Christian history. One Jesus Seminar fan at First Church described the seminar's work as "peeling off the accretions of time"—recovering meanings that have been lost or deemphasized.

At one point in my research, I attended an event called "Stardust, Telescopes, and God." "Stardust" was a publicly advertised event at a Bethel Lutheran retreat center that brought together an astronomer and a professor of religious studies to talk about the night sky. Simon, the religious studies professor, had compiled a list of Biblical excerpts having to do with the night sky. As he interpreted them for the audience, he drew out the metaphorical significance that the words would have had for their original community:

> When the early Jews first started to talk about one god, they called God "sky power"; the idea was this was one god over all other gods. The sky represented the most awesome divine power. . . .
>
> "Can you tie cords to Pleiades, or undo the reins of Orion? Can you lead out the Rooster in its season, conduct the Bear with her sons? Do you know the laws of heaven or impose its authority on earth?" God is that which holds the stars in fixed positions, that's behind the movement of the constellations. They're trying to let God be as big as possible.
>
> "Thy will be done on earth as it is in heaven." This was a Jewish prayer. There was no doubt that the will of God was done in the heavens. They were so orderly. The night sky and the sun by day are metaphors for God. That's where you see the will of God pure, straightforward. Earth is trickier, so "thy will be done on earth, as it is in heaven."
>
> "Holy, holy, holy, is HE-WHO-MAKES-HOSTS-HAPPEN." This is often translated as Host of Hosts, or just Lord, but YHWH was a verb. God is a verb. God is a process. To translate YHWH as "Lord" is a terrible thing to do to it... God as "He" is a terrible translation. The dominant word for God in the Bible is plural. "Elohim, God who is the gods of . . ."
>
> The shepherds' story at Christmas. "Heavenly hosts sang"—that's the stars. The music of the stars—and its message is Shalom! "Hosts" is the word for armies. The stars are the army of God—because of their patterns and orderliness and their marching character.

Simon's exegesis was aimed at making the Bible more meaningful. In effect, he was offering a translation. What would these words have meant in their original community, a small ethnic group in the ancient Middle East? And how can we explain that meaning in language that will make sense to modern Americans?

Jim, in a Common Ground class about the Taoist text the *I Ching*, described this same process of using scholarship to recover lost metaphors:

> The interpretation of the *I Ching* is every bit as difficult as the interpretation of a dream. . . . The *I Ching* gives you poetic images. It's a nugget of essential wisdom. . . . If someone goes to the *I Ching* seeking emergency help, they'll be disappointed. It's for a process of self-understanding. Myth, religion, and dreams are all related. . . . Learning to think symbolically is the key to understanding them. . . . What you'd get from a Jung or a Campbell is they could take us to a deep understanding of the symbolic tradition—the cultural context of the image of, for example, the well—what it connoted in China in 1200 B.C., or through the ages as it was reinterpreted.

This approach to religious texts—understanding them as historically located documents—is not new. For several generations, it has been standard teaching in most U.S. seminaries, where it is called historical criticism, higher criticism, or the historical-critical method. But as we heard Cecil say in Chapter 2, this historical approach often has not made its way from the seminaries to the congregations. With reflexive spirituality, this historical approach is spreading beyond specialists to "the people." By recovering old meanings, reflexive spiritualists find new meaning in the texts of religious tradition.

Responsible Meaning-Making: Using Metaphor Reflexively

We saw earlier that reflexivity brings with it a set of responsibilities, including participating in the renewal of religious tradition and staying patient in the face of ambiguity and discord. Reflexive spiritualists also have a standard for the responsible use of metaphor. To begin with, they consider it important to consciously differentiate metaphors from facts. Cecil, for example, said to one of his classes, "We'll need those symbols, analogies, metaphors, but we'll need to use them in a way that we *realize* we're using a metaphor."

The reason for this self-consciousness about metaphor is the risk of literalization. If we forget that we're using metaphors, we risk taking our stories, images, and words too literally and so losing their rich potential for meaning.

For example, many of the people I observed had become uncomfortable with the word "father" as a way of referring to the divine. In their eyes, overuse had turned "father" into a literal reference that just made people think of an old man. Ron spoke on this subject to a Common Ground class:

> God the Father is not a dogma; it's an image. I was speaking to a group of junior high students once, and the teacher approached me beforehand and said, "Don't refer to 'God the Father,' because some of these kids have really terrible fathers, so that's a bad image for them." And it hit me: "Oh, it's just an image!"

In a radio interview, author Winifred Gallagher made a similar point about the word "god":

> I just heard this morning about a Catholic priest who's going around telling everybody not to use the word "god" because now it's like pressing a button that calls up so many images, and if there's one thing we know about God, it's that anything we could say about God is not right. Because God by definition is indescribable and ineffable.

To get around this problem, reflexive spiritualists like to use a variety of metaphors to refer to the transcendent. At Common Ground, and in many of the public lectures and interviews I attended, speakers made statements that began, "God, Allah, the Tao, Brahman, Unity Consciousness, Christ Consciousness . . ." The implication—which they sometimes made explicit—is that the transcendent reality is what really matters, not the metaphor that we use to refer to it.

Even in the explicitly Christian setting of First Church, reflexive spiritualists like Cecil tried to vary their metaphors. Cecil made this comment to the Theology for the Twenty-First Century class:

> There are many images of God in the Bible, and we've made a lot of some of them. For example, father—we've made a lot of use of that one. But we also see in the Bible God as a mother, and we don't use that very much. I think there's a lot of truth and helpfulness in expanding our imagery.

To reflexive spiritualists, using metaphor responsibly means remembering that no matter what words they use in their "god talk," those words never fully capture the nature of the transcendent. Instead, words offer familiar images that people can use to explore, express, and imagine the transcendent. Reflexive spiritualists see the transcendent as ineffable and infinitely meaningful, and they don't want to limit its meaningfulness by getting too attached to any one set of images. So they mine religious traditions to increase their spiritual vocabulary and practice using a variety of metaphors to speak and think about the transcendent.

Pluralism: All Religions Are Meaningful

> I saw the Buddha open up his eyes
> One Sunday morning
> Say he's invited to a party for Christ
> And he must be going
> He heaved himself up with a groan, standing slowly,
> Came down his steps of stone, and asked me
> Where to catch the next train to Jerusalem
>
> In India he sang with Hindus as they prayed
> By the Ganges when the dawn came
> Near Arabia, he saw Mohammed on the train
> And asked if he would join him
> Passing those teeming towns, they talked for hours
> All about the truth and how it's discovered
> Trading bits of news and stories from these thousand years,
> Saying, "great idea, this party for Jesus"
> Then Mohammed said, "hey Buddha, it's great to see ya"
>
> Finding the place with the help of Abraham
> Waving from the doorway
> They greeted faces from a thousand holy lands
> From present day and all ages
> Everybody talking, laughing, fiercely debating
> Saying how desperately the world is changing
> Then somebody lit the two thousand candles
> And they all toasted Jesus, born in a stable
> And Jesus said, "hey let's not be such strangers"
>
> Peter Mayer, *The Birthday Party*[12]

Before the world became so small—before modern travel and communication—any society could think of its religion as simply "the way," "the truth," and the only alternative to chaos, amorality, and meaninglessness. But in the modern world, we know about a lot of ways, a lot of truths, a lot of religions, spiritualities, and philosophies. Even if we don't know much about them, we know that they're there. We know there are other people, maybe people in our neighborhood, whose religious commitments, beliefs, and practices are different from our own.

One way to respond to the multiplicity of religions and spiritualities in the world is with *exclusivism*: we can dig in our heels and insist that our way is the right way, our beliefs are the truth, and other religions are inferior. Alternatively, we might respond with *rejection* and conclude that all religions are essentially delusional—after all, they all promote different beliefs that conflict not only with one another but also with a purely scientific worldview.

Reflexive spirituality offers a third response: *pluralism*. In the face of more than four thousand religious traditions around the world, reflexive spiritualists suspect that probably, each one of them has some purchase on the truth. More importantly, each one of them offers its own history of spiritual insight and wisdom, so each one could be a valid and valuable source of transcendent meaning. The world's religions become a treasure chest of meaning, a mansion with thousands of different windows to the divine, a nearly endless set of resources for wisdom, insight, and truth.

Reflexivity and metaphor make religious pluralism possible. When all traditions are revisable, then none of them have the complete truth. When "all knowledge takes the form of hypotheses," then all religions get to be different, potentially worthwhile sources of good hypotheses about transcendent meaning. And when we're listening for rich metaphors rather than singular facts, then all religions can speak to us of truth.

Pluralism reminds me of students or scholars composing a scholarly argument. We start with a topic, research a variety of credible sources to find what's already known about that topic, and then make an original argument that draws on those multiple sources but goes beyond them. With pluralism, the topic is the transcendent. What's already known about the transcendent lies in the world's religious traditions, and reflexive spiritualists draw on these traditions as resources in their own search for transcendent meaning.

Paths to the Center: All Religions Are Valid and Important

The *Rig Veda*, an ancient Hindu text, says, "Truth is one, but the sages call it by different names." William Shakespeare, in *Romeo and Juliet*, asked, "What's in a name? That which we call a rose / By any other name would smell as sweet." Mythologist Joseph Campbell, in the many interviews he gave, often warned that if we don't look beyond religious symbols to their larger meaning, then we are like "diners going into a restaurant and eating the menu."

The *Rig Veda*, Shakespeare, and Campbell are all talking about language—they're all distinguishing between the language we use and the truths that language points to. Language, they're saying, is imperfect. It can't contain truth; it can only refer us to truth, remind us of truth, suggest truth, point to truth.[13]

Reflexive spiritualists think of religion this way. There is no one correct religion, just as there is no one correct language; both religion and language give us different ways of talking about truths that lie beyond language. At Common Ground, Ron made this comparison explicitly:

> One's religion is one's own experience of how one is connected to the divine. For my whole life, my link to the divine has been in the person of Jesus. It's just like saying, "I've spoken English since I was a kid." It's not a position from which to judge. When I say I'm a Christian, I'm saying Christianity is the language that gives me the vocabulary to experience the divine. We don't say French is deficient English. French is a valid language; it does what languages do. The different religious traditions all do what religions need to do, which is produce holiness.

This distinction between religion and holiness is the key to pluralism. In a pluralist perspective, the different religions of the world are equally legitimate "paths to the center"—each can lead to the transcendent, but none can contain it. The transcendent—the divine—is just too big for any one religion to completely capture it. Religious pluralists see each path as valid, even while they follow their own. At Common Ground, for example, Ron described a pluralistic Christianity as one that sees Jesus as a path to the divine, not as the totality of the divine:

> Jesus is a window to the divine mystery. Jesus is the way Christians apprehend the divine mystery, what Christians call God, what in Eastern religions is called Tao, or Dharma. Jesus is the way Christians apprehend the divine mystery, just as Muslims apprehend the divine mystery through the Koran, Jews apprehend the divine mystery through the Torah. The world religions are ways to the center, ways to the experience of the holy.

Wayne, another Common Ground teacher, spoke of pluralism in a similar way: he told one of his classes, "All traditions are valid; all lead to the same place: holiness. . . . It's all one tradition because it all comes from the same source, but it's filtered through different cultures, languages, histories."

For reflexive spiritualists, the idea of multiple paths to the divine doesn't devalue any particular path. In fact, the opposite is true: they tend to take the universality of religion as prima facie evidence that all religions are speaking to truth. Common Ground's Ron and Jim, for example, told their students to think of different religions as evidence for a larger truth, rather than as competing truths:

RON: A Catholic priest came to speak to one of my classes, and he said, "Okay, let's start with something we can all agree on: If one religion is true, then all the others are false." I said, "I can see it's gonna be a long night because that's not something we all agree on. I would say instead that if one religion is true, then chances are they're all true."

JIM: Imagine only one valid, true form of art. It's bizarre and silly.

SARAH: Didn't Jesus say, "Only by me do you reach the Father"?

RON: I like to think of it as mutual irradiation of religions. Religions illuminate each other. You get to nirvana by the Buddha, you get to the Father by Jesus. These are symbols, and mixing the symbols doesn't make sense.

Jim's comparison between religion and art is telling. Art is a symbolic form of communication, one that sparks the imagination and comprehends ideas and emotions that can't be expressed in ordinary language. New art is always called for as human beings constantly seek new ways of orienting ourselves to life's challenges and joys. Artists build on artistic tradition through creativity and innovation. Different communities produce different kinds of art, and once in a while, great art transcends its own time and local context to inspire succeeding generations around the world. If religion is like art, then all religions are worth exploring because all are potential sources of transcendent meaning, wisdom, and spiritual truth.

In light of ongoing religious distrust and violence, pluralism feels urgent to reflexive spiritualists; it feels like a way of healing interreligious divisiveness. During a Spirituality at Work Dialogue with Jack Shea, for example, one man spoke of how religious differences separated people in his childhood:

As a kid, where I grew up, it was Roman Catholics, Protestants, Jews, and other folks. [He motions with his hands as he's talking, placing each religious group in a different space.] It was "those guys," instead of "us." Over the past forty years, there's been this development, we're really all talking about the same stuff, we all have a notion of divine presence, we just have different paths to get there. Maybe that's what we need to get beyond that.

At a public lecture, a large audience applauded as author Neale Walsch promoted pluralism as a means of preventing violence:

> What has caused so much violence is the idea, taught by most religions, that *my* way is the *only* way. Because *God told us!* There are 268 known religions on the planet. So either there are 268 gods, telling everyone something different, or we're confused somewhere. Religion isn't taught like "we think this is a good way"; it's taught like "this is *the* way to *save your soul!*" . . . God said to me, "Challenge all leaders to teach: Ours is not a better way, ours is merely *another* way to God."

Neale Walsch's lecture and Jack Shea's Dialogues were nonsectarian events, and Common Ground is an explicitly interfaith adult education center, and pluralism may feel especially natural in these kinds of settings. But pluralism does not prevent people from identifying with a particular religious tradition.[14] First Church stands firmly within the tradition of mainline Protestant Christianity. Naturally, First Church members spent most of their time discussing Christianity. But within that context, leaders still promoted a pluralistic attitude toward other religious traditions. In one sermon, for example, David rejected exclusivistic versions of Christianity and drew on the Bible to make his case:

> Just last week, someone asked me what I thought about other religions, about people of other religions. The question was, can they be saved? Is Jesus the only way? I answer "Yes" and "No." For me, he is the only way. Because I was brought up in a Christian Church, in a Christian culture, my parents were Christian—that's the language they spoke—I've read the Bible and studied Christianity. I haven't read the Bhagavad Gita, I haven't read the Koran, I haven't read the other sacred scriptures. So for me, Jesus is the way.
>
>   But will others of other faiths find salvation? Can they, without Jesus, be saved? Yes. Is Jesus the only way for *all* people? I give an emphatic, emphatic *No.*

I can't help thinking of Moses and the burning bush, and he asked God, "What is your name?" And God said, I'm not gonna let you put me in that box. "I am that I am," or I think of it, "I will be present as I will be present." You can't put God in a box.

Members of David's congregation shared his views. In the Theology for the Twenty-First Century class, for example, Jerry's pluralism helped him oppose anti-Semitism and imagine a more expansive god:

I once heard a bishop say that God doesn't hear Jews' prayers. So either God is a two-bit deity undeserving of anybody's attention, or this bishop is a two-bit preacher undeserving of anybody's attention, and God is a little more than that.

A member of the Faith and Reason group used pluralism to find spiritual meaning beyond the Bible-centeredness of Protestant tradition:

What I hate is when people hold up a Bible and say, "It's all right here." I look, and I don't find it all there. I like to think it's an open book and it's in other places together with there.

Cecil voiced opinions similar to David's; he told the Reading the Bible Intelligently class, "We can know how God has spoken to us, but we can't know that God hasn't spoken to others in other ways." Cecil taught an ongoing adult Sunday School class called Religions of the World that used Huston Smith's popular textbook of the same name. He began one meeting, on Buddhism, with these words:

Our purpose in this class is to appreciate the spirituality of another people and the deep kinship we have with people with other points of view. . . . One of our reactions to Buddhism as Christians is, "There's no god—that's not religion as I know it." When I was in school, we studied Buddhism. Our teachers didn't say explicitly we were studying it in order to convert them, but that was the underlying—We were studying it from the standpoint of "We have the one true faith and those poor saps don't have it right."

At this point, a woman named Jill spoke up. She described herself as a "Methodist Buddhist" and said, "For me, the thing about not having a god is how do we limit God by giving it a name. I think the kinds of god you can get in Buddhism and Christianity are similar. The mystical parts of Christianity and Buddhism recognize each other well." Jill, like other reflexive spiritualists, thinks of the different religious traditions as different attempts to articulate a phenomenon that is beyond articulation. As a Christian, the idea of God is important to her. But her investigations into Buddhism have helped her imagine God in new, more expansive ways. For Jill and other pluralists, the differences between religions are not negative or divisive, but positive and creative. They spark the imagination, nurture insight, and evoke ever-greater transcendent meaning.

United Against a Common Enemy

In a society dominated by technical reason, the very idea of a transcendent reality can be countercultural. As Chapters 3 and 4 explained, technical reason just can't make sense of the idea of transcendent meaning. In a society dominated by technical reason, people face a constant risk of meaninglessness, a feeling of emptiness, a feeling that after all, there is nothing more in life than what technological reason allows us to see.

Against this backdrop, reflexive spiritualists sometimes approach the world's religions as an arsenal in the fight against meaninglessness—various weapons they can draw to insist that there is more to life than meets the eye. Most reflexive spiritualists recognize that there are significant differences between religions, that it's not quite as simple as "they're all just saying the same thing."[15] At the same time, religions' similarities are what most interest reflexive spiritualists. After all, one thing all religions have in common is their ability to endow life with transcendent meaning. When different religions seem to support each other, the case for meaning seems somehow stronger.

So reflexive spiritualists often drew together comparable insights from different religious traditions. For example, during a Common Ground discussion of Thomas Moore's book *The Education of the Heart*, one participant said that her favorite quote from the book was theologian Paul Tillich's words, "You are accepted." She said,

> Just accept that you're accepted. Don't worry about it; you don't have to do anything differently to be enlightened. It's like "Every being has Buddha nature." It's like "The kingdom is within you."

And Ron, in another class, said, "I like the idea of purgatory because I see it as parallel to reincarnation—both acknowledge the ongoingness of life, in which a kind of cleansing takes place."

Sometimes, instead of making explicit comparisons like that, reflexive spiritualists simply made blanket statements along the lines of "all traditions have this idea," to help them make the point that the idea was an important one. So at Common Ground, Jim said, "Every tradition has a symbol that combines the circle and the square. There is no tradition without this symbol of the interplay of the one and the many, unity and separateness." And Ron said, "In the Tao, Buddhists, the Gospels too, all say that you can't get forgiveness without giving forgiveness. This is not a rule; it's a circumstance. Life is just set up that way."

In his Callings workshop, Gregg Levoy told participants to pay attention to their dreams, saying, "All religions of the world agree that dreams are primary channels through which the gods speak to mortals." In a public lecture, author Parker Palmer told his audience, "Virtually every spiritual tradition tells us that if we are willing to contemplate death . . . we will enter into life more earnestly and with more energy and joy." During a radio interview, Winifred Gallagher was asked how to keep from getting self-centered in a spiritual search. She said:

> All the great religious traditions say, yes, there is the sacred, and you want to have your prayer life or your meditative life, your private spiritual life that's involved with your relationship to this sacred thing. Right away, go outside and help your neighbor. It's a universal message, and any religion that tells you that it's all about you you you, I think is questionable.

This sense of bringing different religions together in support of shared ideas was stronger in interfaith settings such as Common Ground than in settings focused on a single tradition, such as First Church. It was strongest of all in secular settings, where reflexive spiritualists couldn't take for granted that the people they were talking to had any value for transcendent meaning. And it was most pressing in the Spirit-at-Work movement, for which the corporate environment and its institutionalized technological rationality were a constant background presence.[16] So in his dialogues with business people, Jack Shea took this distillation process to an extreme by referring to "spiritual traditions" as one collective voice:

People are searching for meaning at work. Spiritual traditions have a lot to say about meaning, how meaning is created, how to recognize the meaning of your work. . . . Last time, we talked about stress, outer-world stressors and inner-world stressors. . . . It's typical of spiritual traditions, you work with the inside to effect change on the outside. . . . Spiritual traditions are often contrary, unconventional ways of thinking. One of the things they think is misguided is that we think development takes place by doing more—accumulation. They think more and more makes us more cluttered. Do less, and your essence or soul shines forth. . . . Spiritual traditions have practices to bring balance, practices to stay in touch with deeper or vital centers.

Often, especially in more secular settings, people extended the idea of religious pluralism to embrace secular sources of wisdom, too. Meaning can be found in a lot of places, and a speaker who had an hour or two to make an extended point might refer to twenty or thirty different sources to illustrate and defend that point. For example, Wayne Dyer's two-hour televised talk "Improving Your Life Using the Wisdom of the Ages" was an extended argument in which the main point was, in effect, "There really is a spiritual dimension to life," and secondary points had to do with the wisdom of recognizing, identifying, and living from a spiritual center. To make these fundamental points, Dyer drew on Socrates, the Buddha, Jesus, the Hindu sage Patanjali, Michelangelo, Keats, Yeats, Shelley, da Vinci, Martin Luther King, Jr., Mother Teresa, Aldous Huxley, the Taoist sage Lao-tzu, Emily Dickinson, Herman Melville, Robert Frost, a variety of Zen proverbs, the Sufi poet Talopa, Blaise Pascal, the novel *The Legend of Bagger Vance*, Saint Paul, Emerson, and Thoreau. Gregg Levoy drew on a similarly long list of sources in the course of his Callings workshop, and Common Ground teachers drew on similar lists that typically included more scholars and fewer poets.

The point to bringing together similar ideas from different religious, philosophical, and literary traditions is not to gloss over these traditions' differences by pretending they're all identical. The point is to fight against meaninglessness. The point is that in a society that focuses our attention on surfaces, the world's religious traditions remind us that depths still exist, that they matter, and that we can learn to live from a deeper, more meaningful place.

The Blind Men and the Elephant

Religion can be many things: a lifestyle, a system of beliefs, a ritual calendar, a cultural identity, a political stance, a shared vocabulary, a set of moral commitments, a guide for behavior, a tool for belonging, a worldview. Transcendent meaning isn't the only thing religion offers—but for reflexive spiritualists, it's the thing that matters most of all. The sacred, the holy, the transcendent—this is the heart of what religious traditions are about for reflexive spiritualists. So when reflexive spiritualists look at the differences between religious traditions, they tend to divide these differences into two broad categories: those that speak seriously to issues of transcendent meaning, and those that don't.

"Those that don't" include differences that seem to be mostly about language and culture. Reflexive spiritualists see all religious language as ultimately inadequate to truly capture the ineffable reality of the transcendent. To reflexive spiritualists, many differences in religious traditions seem, at root, to be different ways of trying to talk about something that's ultimately beyond expression. Wayne Dyer put it this way in a televised lecture:

> There is an energy in the universe, there is something that is in each and every one of us, and it's also in the universe, and you are connected to it . . . And it doesn't matter what you call it, if you call it God, Divine Presence, Soul, Spirit, Consciousness, Christ Consciousness, Buddha Consciousness. You can't get wet from the word *water*—experiencing it is different from what you call it. Kierkegaard said, "Once you label me, you negate me."

Reflexive spiritualists see different religious vocabularies as representing different understandings of the transcendent, and they might investigate these different understandings. But ultimately, what interests them most is the transcendent reality to which all the different vocabularies point. They assume that each word for the transcendent is ultimately inadequate, so they don't invest their energy in arguing over the best or truest words to use—those kinds of arguments seem to them to be little more than quibbles over terminology.

Religious doctrine and ritual come off as slightly more important, but still not fundamental for the meaning-seeking individual. For reflexive spiritualists, doctrine and ritual are more about culture than they are about God. They're culturally created vehicles meant to help people relate to the transcendent, and they're important to the extent that they successfully do that. But the fact that different religions promote different doctrines and rituals isn't a problem for reflexive spiritualists, because neither doctrine nor ritual is what they're most looking for.

What they're most looking for, of course, is transcendent meaning, and some religious differences do have to do with transcendent meaning. In these cases, reflexive spiritualists compare different religious traditions to the classic story of blind men trying to describe an elephant. In the story, each man is touching a different part of an elephant, and so each describes the elephant differently: "It's like a rope," says the man feeling the tail. "It's like a pipe," says the man feeling the tusk. "It's like the branch of a tree," says the man feeling the trunk. For reflexive spiritualists, different religions are feeling different parts of the elephant of transcendence, and each has it right, but none has it completely right. Wayne voiced this perspective at Common Ground:

> A big question for religions is not "Which is truer?" but "How are they all true?" Like the blind man and the elephant, the bigger truth is when you put it all together. Different religions complete each other; the strengths in each complement the weaknesses in the others. So for example, Jainists' reverence for life, Western Christianity's social engagement, the Eastern contemplative tradition, the nature religions' unity with nature.

In practice, many reflexive spiritualists do draw on multiple religions to help complete their spiritual worldview. One common example is Christians and Jews embracing the idea of reincarnation; many reflexive spiritualists find that the idea of reincarnation helps them find meaning in suffering.

Another way reflexive spiritualists address religious difference is comparing and contrasting specific religious ideas to try to make sense of a particular problem. At Common Ground, for example, Jim contrasted different ways of making sense of illness, ending with a Buddhist approach that made the most sense to him:

> We evolve this tendency to outcast the ill person. It's either visited on us by God or by our self. In Christianity, illness gets seen as God's punishment; in the New Age movement, it's your failure, you're clinging to something or something, or you've called the illness to you for your own development. In Buddhism, it just is. You respond.

At the Stardust, Telescopes, and God event, a participant asked Simon, the religious studies professor, to describe ideas in other religions that might compare to the Christian idea of resurrection. Andrew spoke of Egyptian and Jewish traditions:

> The Egyptians got into "Life goes on." In the third millennium B.C., souls locate in birds before moving into a new body. The Jewish tradition emphasized your life goes on in your descendants. The most religious word in the Jewish tradition is "remember." The great ritual is remembering the dead. Living on as an influence. You live on as you are remembered, your teachings and whatever you stood for. Also genetically. You carry your ancestors with you.

Lists like these can be about choosing from among different options: which approach to illness or life after death is most meaningful to me? More often, though, these kinds of lists are an effort to illuminate similar ideas by reflecting on them as variations on a theme.

Reflexive spiritualists don't ignore differences between religions. But their emphasis is not on locating the boundaries between religions and preserving each religion's unique identity. They find more meaning in connections. They want to bring different religious ideas into communication with each other to help them in their own search for meaning. Some reflexive spiritualists are suspicious of what they call "pick and choose" approaches to religious diversity out of a concern that picking and choosing can degenerate into shallowness and egotism. But the difference between "picking and choosing" and true pluralism is one of degree: both are about mining wisdom wherever it can be found instead of holding fast to one tradition and rejecting or ignoring wisdom that comes from other places. For reflexive spiritualists, the different religions of the world offer different perspectives, and combining these perspectives makes for a richer, more dimensional picture of the transcendent.

Mysticism: Religion Is About Experience, Not Belief

Reflexive spiritualists get excited about the connections and similarities they find between different religions. It makes intuitive sense to them that if different religions address the same topic or offer the same message, then that topic or message is probably especially important and meaningful—that it probably speaks especially deeply of transcendent reality and human experience.

This process of lifting up the big ideas that religions have in common gives reflexive spiritualists a special interest in *mysticism*: direct experience of the transcendent. All religions have a tradition of practices, such as prayer and meditation, that are designed to help people develop an experiential connection with God, the divine, or ultimate reality. And all the major religions have a lineage of people who have written or spoken about their experiences of transcendence. These descriptions are remarkably similar across different traditions—a fact noted more than a century ago by psychologist William James in his book *The Varieties of Religious Experience*.

The sifting-and-distilling action of pluralism leads reflexive spiritualists to see mysticism as something that all religions agree on. Mysticism, then, comes to seem like the core and the heart of religion. Reflexive spiritualists are in search of meaning, and the meanings associated with mysticism are especially compelling in part because they appear so consistently in such a wide variety of traditions.

In modern society, the word "mysticism" connotes something totally irrational. The meanings that a society gives to a word are recorded in its dictionaries, and one of Webster's definitions of mysticism is "a vague speculation: a belief without sound basis." But a long tradition of scholarship has linked mysticism with intellectual reason.[17] And in many ways, mysticism resonates strongly with intellectual rationality.

At a basic level, mysticism seems to come with a lot of evidence, insofar as sheer repetition from unconnected sources counts as evidence. Because all religions have a mystical tradition, and because these traditions all resonate so strongly with one another, reflexive spiritualists find it difficult to believe that there's just nothing to it, that it's all "without sound basis," no matter how difficult it is to understand from the narrow vantage point of technological reason.

Mysticism also resonates with the modern tradition of *empiricism*: the practice, which lies at the foundation of science, of acquiring knowledge through systematic observation and experience. Wayne made this connection during a class at Common Ground:

> At the core of all religious traditions is a mystical experience, an experience of unity, of oneness, with the divine. And all of us, all people, are meant for that experience. We are all mystics, that's our nature. You don't have to take my word for it. It's not a question of faith. It's a question of experience. Just *look*. Mysticism is more empirical than science. You get a total view, and it's your direct experience. Prayers, meditation, yoga, tai chi, all these are about awakening that.

As we've seen, reflexive spiritualists have a modern consciousness of the limits of religious language; they separate words from truth. Religious texts, then, come across in part as attempts to describe the inherently indescribable experience of transcendence. To put it more simply, reflexive spiritualists see religions as records of people's experiences of God. The language—the scriptures, doctrines, prayers, and rules—is secondary. What's primary is the experience of the transcendent—the experience of God. At best, scriptures, doctrines, and prayers serve as tools or guideposts to help people build an experiential connection with the divine.

Many reflexive spiritualists think of mysticism as both the intersection and the origin of the world's religions. Common Ground's Wayne was especially interested in mysticism, and he described it like this:

> There's the metaphor of a hand: the five major religions are distinct fingers, but they come together at the palm, which represents the mystical dimension....
>
> Religion is an attempt to institutionalize moments of spiritual insight. The founders of all the great religions were mystics. The origin of all the religious traditions is people flocking to individuals who've had incredible breakthroughs. This is certainly true of Buddhism, and likely of Hinduism.... Then in the Biblical tradition, the whole tradition depends on a long line of individuals who have an intimate mystical relationship to the divine.
>
> The basic purpose of religion is to preserve what has been gained in these mystical experiences, and pass them on.

Reflexive spiritualists' interest in mysticism plays out in two ways, one having to do with their own personal spiritual experience and the other having to do with the theologies of religious traditions. To cultivate their own experiential connection with the divine, reflexive spiritualists engage in spiritual practices and talk with one another about what spiritual experience is and what experiences they and the people they know have had. When they turn to religious tradition, they pay special attention to theologies associated with mysticism. I want to talk first about reflexive spiritualists' emphasis on experience, and then turn to the ways this emphasis helps them find meaning in religion.

Spiritual Experience and Spiritual Practice

For reflexive spiritualists, spiritual experience gives life. Many spoke of it as liberating, as bringing new vitality to both life and religion. First Church members, for example, spoke of "experiencing God's presence" or "experiencing the Holy Spirit," and connected this experience with energy. David spoke in one sermon about the vitality and power of the Holy Spirit:

> In talking about the Holy Spirit, the church doesn't begin with a definition. It begins with an experience—the experience of Pentecost. . . . According to Luke in Acts, the disciples at Pentecost had an unusual experience. . . . They began to speak in unfamiliar languages and tongues, and could talk to all the pilgrims from all the many lands, such that all could be understood. Luke attributes that experience to the Holy Spirit.
>
> Through the Holy Spirit, the routine becomes exciting, the powerless becomes powerful. The Holy Spirit brings to life and existence a dynamism. Dynamic. The word Luke uses is Greek and it translates to "power." That's the word most frequently associated with the Holy Spirit in the New Testament. . . .
>
> The Holy Spirit allows us to be more than we have been. The same spirit that descended like a dove on the shoulders of a Galilean peasant, and empowered him to change the face of history, can work in us too. We must be open to change—the Holy Spirit changes things, makes us expand beyond where we were before. But if we are open, we'll experience life as we have never experienced it before.

For author Winifred Gallagher, spiritual experience led her, in midlife, to begin to identify as a Christian after an agnostic young adulthood and several years exploring other religious traditions. Because she came to Christianity through spiritual experience, her understanding of the religion is very different from the belief-centered version she learned in childhood:

> I've come to trust in my own experience of the sacred. Which is different from saying "I believe in the virgin birth" or "I believe that Jesus Christ was God." It's a lot different kind of starting place for religion, and I think one that speaks to a lot of people. . . .
>
> For me, Jesus is a vivid presence, and that's why I'm a Christian. . . . My definition of Christianity is a living experience of Jesus, so that I have an experiential definition of Christianity, as opposed to my mom's definition of Christianity, which is contained in the Apostles' Creed.

Because reflexive spiritualists find spiritual experience so important, they often pursue disciplined spiritual practices designed to cultivate this experience.

Common Ground teachers were tireless in their promotion of meditation; Ron, in particular, often said things like "Americans need to learn to be quiet. We have to be quiet in order to hear." For Ron, a practice is the key to transforming a spiritual *experience* into a spiritual *life*:

> What's the difference between having a mystical experience and leading a mystical life? So it isn't just a mystical high, a temporary thing, but really integrated into my life? In *certain* parts of the New Age, they're just cultivating experience—go and get another high and then go home, and next weekend go and get another spiritual high and go home. That's not spirituality. That's like a spiritual masturbation. There's the striking of the match, and then there's the steadfast burning. . . . What's involved in the movement from mystical experience to mystical life is a steadfast commitment to practice.

Author Gregg Levoy, speaking to business people, broadened the idea of practice beyond meditation and prayer. For Gregg, a spiritual practice might be any reflective ritual that offers an alternative to the assumptions of technological rationality:

> In my book research, I found that many of my interviewees had a practice that kept them in touch with this, a sophisticated, regular practice. A calling is half a conversation, and you must be in dialogue with it. Practices included journaling, meditation, therapy, a dream log. . . . Artwork as self-discovery. Contemplative reading—so *in addition* to reading *Fortune* and *Newsweek*, you *also* are reading wisdom books. You keep one foot in the mortal world and one in the sacred, one foot in the outer and one in the inner, one foot in competence and the other in authenticity. Another practice: group membership, people gather for the purpose of *awakening*. Twelve-step groups, church group, therapy group. This builds accountability into this piece of your life. This activity builds accountability into your life.

Sociologists who study religion have made the same point. Robert Wuthnow, for example, describes practice as a way to make sure that spiritual exploration is disciplined, grounded, and centered, rather than chaotic, shallow, and selfish.[18]

Revitalizing Religious Tradition

Religious leaders and scholars sometimes distrust mysticism. They worry that all this talk of personal spiritual experience will result in a nation of isolated individuals, all shut up in their respective closets, gazing at their navels—or their third eyes. What will happen to religious community, and what will happen to religious traditions that have been sculpted and honed over thousands of years? Will they simply be lost as people focus in on their own inner worlds?[19]

For reflexive spiritualists, mysticism is not only about exploring the inner spiritual world—it's also about interacting with tradition. Mysticism offers a *renewal* of tradition, and just as it brings vitality to life, it can also revitalize religion. Mysticism helps reflexive spiritualists renew religious tradition in three main ways.

First, reflexive spiritualists see mystical experience as the origin, the heart, and the reason for religion. To them, the world religions came about because of the extraordinary insight and courage of people who had had mystical experiences: God telling Abraham to leave his native land and go to a new place, Moses arguing with an unnamable holy voice that spoke to him from a burning bush, Jesus praying in the hills to a god he called "papa," the Buddha becoming enlightened under the bodhi tree, an angel telling Mohammad to "recite" and giving him the first verses of the Koran. Reflexive spiritualists are interested in religions' mystical origins, and they want to see religious traditions give these mystical origins greater prominence. They want religious communities to pay attention to Jesus more than the Pauline church, to Moses's experience on Mount Sinai more than the Ten Commandments, to Mohammed's experience of hearing the voice of God more than Islamic law, and to the words of Lao-tzu, Chuang-tzu, the Buddha, and the Hindu yogis more than the dictates of orthopraxy. By returning to mysticism and the insights of these founding mystics, reflexive spiritualists hope to highlight the most original and important dimension of religious traditions. Ron drew on William James's *Varieties of Religious Experience* to describe this logic:

> James refers to firsthand and secondhand religion. He describes an experience of the divine as central to all religion. That's where you catch religion at its purest, at the source. Then it starts doing what all human things do. Firsthand religion, A, is Jesus fresh from the forty days and forty nights, or the Buddha just after enlightenment. Secondhand religion, B, helps recapitulate the divine experience of firsthand religion.

Then we get down to C, D, and E, and you get to people killing each other over whether X or Y was right, and A has been forgotten. I had a student from Thailand once who said that for her, "Buddhism is just my grandmother lighting incense sticks." That's the danger of religion.[20]

Ron's concern resonates with reflexive spirituality's overall interest in getting to the heart of the matter, getting to the depths, getting to what's most meaningful. He hopes that a return to mysticism will put people closer to the core of religion. Mysticism is direct experience of the divine, and for Ron and other reflexive spiritualists, the insight that comes from that experience is the heart of religion and what religious traditions should be working to retain.

A second way that mysticism helps reflexive spiritualists renew religious tradition is by giving them a personal, experiential connection with it. Spiritual experiences can bring new meaning to the sometimes obscure language of religious traditions. In turn, religious traditions offer people a language with which to think about and make sense of their spiritual experiences. The result is an ongoing dialogue between personal experience and religious tradition that reflexive spiritualists find much more compelling and satisfying than the insight they might get from simply listening to and obeying religious authorities. Wayne, for example, told his Common Ground students that they would find more depth and resonance in their exploration of religious traditions if they participated in a spiritual practice, and his student Ann agreed with him:

WAYNE: Mysticism is the origin of religion. All religions come out of a primary experience of the divine.... We must approach the traditions from a very deep commitment to your own spiritual life. That practice then allows you to get in touch with a very deep base. That gives you a foundation to explore, so all your explorations are illuminated by and illuminating of your practice. Yeah. It gives you a platform, a foundation from which you can explore religious tradition, not superficially.

ANN: 'Cause you can recognize your experience in all these traditions.

When people participate in a spiritual practice, Wayne and Ann are saying, they see religious tradition with new eyes. The scriptures and rituals of the tradition come to make sense, not so much because they seem logical, but because they resonate with personal experience and seem to speak to the human–divine relationship—just as a love song makes sense because it captures a piece of what it's like to be in love, or a novel makes sense because it reminds us of our own life stories.

The third way mysticism helps reflexive spiritualists renew religious tradition has to do with the fact that mysticism is itself a tradition. Mysticism is a sub-tradition of all the world religions. So when reflexive spiritualists emphasize mysticism, they're not opposing religious tradition but rather highlighting an aspect of religious tradition that different religions have in common. Reflexive spiritualists are interested in meaning, and they mine mystical traditions for the transcendent meanings they offer. In other words, reflexive spiritualists are interested in mystical theology—statements about the nature of the transcendent that come from the spiritual experiences of mystics.

For example, mystical traditions uniformly emphasize human communion with the divine. Mystics throughout history and around the world insist, based on their experience, that there is an existential connection that unites us with the divine and with each other, and that we can experience this connection as a kind of intimacy with the divine. So at a Common Ground summer retreat, Jim told his students, "'You are God' is the big mystical secret of all religions." Ron made the same point during a discussion of the book *Minyan*, by Rabbi Rami Shapiro:

> We are manifestations of the divine. The rhythm of the universe, the rhythm of life, is from unmanifest to manifest; it all comes out of and goes back to the godhead—the return to the source. You find this message in all mystics. I'm reading about a Jewish Orthodox mystic, I'm also reading about the Sufi tradition, and you find this idea there. It's a perennial philosophy. We are God, but not the totality of God. In Quakerism, to be a Quaker, the only dogma is "There is that of God in everyone." The "Namaste" greeting in Hinduism: the god in me greets the god in you. Jewish, Christian, Muslim, Buddhist, Hindu: If there is any universal teaching, this is it.

With these words, Ron is renewing religious tradition. He's highlighting a theological message that's common to the mystical traditions in all religions and saying, essentially, "What if we think about God this way?" Ultimately, as always in reflexive spirituality, the point is to infuse life with transcendent meaning. If we think of human beings as expressions of God, then we infuse every encounter and every relationship with a larger meaning—with divine significance.

Reflexivity, metaphor, pluralism, and mysticism all draw on our modern heritage of intellectual reason. These are tools for thinking, tools for reflecting, tools of criticism, tools of inquiry. And in the hands of reflexive spiritualists, all are tools for making meaning. Reflexive spiritualists use these tools to "make religion speak to them"—to make religion reveal the transcendent meaning it's designed to communicate.

I've touched only briefly in this chapter on the specific transcendent meanings that reflexive spiritualists come up with when they look at religion. For example, their interest in mysticism and mystical theology leads reflexive spiritualists to think of the divine and the human as one, or as intimately connected on an existential level. In the next chapter, I delve more deeply into the other transcendent meanings that are most central to reflexive spiritualists: the popular theology that all their spiritual work points to.

6 THE GOD OF REFLEXIVE SPIRITUALITY

Beyond the desert of criticism, we wish to be called again.

—PAUL RICOEUR[1]

What is God like? What's the nature of ultimate reality? What is the relationship between the divine and the ordinary world? Why bother with a notion of God, transcendence, or spiritual reality? What is the meaning of life, the universe, and everything, anyway?

Like other people interested in spirituality, reflexive spiritualists spend time thinking and talking about these kinds of ultimate questions. What they arrive at is a popular theology—a set of statements about the nature of the transcendent. They're not trying to offer a comprehensive definition of God; in fact, they see that kind of thing as impossible. But in their god-talk, they do emphasize particular qualities of the divine. When the reflexive spiritualists I studied talked about God, the transcendent, or the divine, they described it as *infinite*, *immanent*, and *vitalizing*. I heard these three themes over and over; these were the qualities of the divine that were most important in all the settings I studied. And not surprisingly, each of these qualities speaks directly to the problem of meaning in modern society.

Most of this chapter describes these three themes in detail, but first, I want to talk about another piece of this theological package. The theology of reflexive spirituality has an energy to it, an emotional sensibility, that's just as much a part of this spirituality as the more intellectual qualities that I discuss throughout the book. Reflexive spirituality's intellectual tone might be its most obvious quality, but spirituality isn't just something that people think about—it's something people *feel*.

The Project of Divinity

Back in 1980, the German social theorist Jurgen Habermas delivered a talk called "Modernity—An Incomplete Project." Other sociologists picked up on Habermas's ideas and began to write about "the unfinished project of modernity." In a nutshell, the project of modernity is the ongoing work of constructing a society built on reason—the effort to make a society that answers to our human capacity for reason. Reflexive spirituality is part of the project of modernity. Reflexive spiritualists are seeking to bring religion and spirituality into the fold of rationality, so to speak—they want a spirituality that makes sense to them intellectually.

But a reasonable spirituality is not all that reflexive spiritualists want. As we've seen, reflexive spiritualists are critical of narrow rationalisms that place limits on what we can think of as real or possible or true. They experience technological rationality, for example, as more constraining than liberating, because it doesn't leave room for anything but the narrowly reasonable. Emotion, intuition, inspiration—these things are all incomprehensible from a strict rationalist standpoint, yet they're an essential part of human life. So reflexive spiritualists don't want to just harness religion and rationalize it. They see that kind of thing as falling flat—creating the kinds of distortions I described in Chapter 4.

Reflexive spiritualists are engaged in what I've taken to calling "the project of divinity"—the project of creating a society that answers to our human capacity for transcendent meaning. Reflexive spiritualists want a society that cultivates insight into higher truths, where "truth" is not *fact*—sealed-up answers to life's eternal questions—but *possibility*, an eternal question about purpose and significance. They want us to lift our eyes to a higher horizon, to see more deeply, and to act based on wisdom. This is one way that reflexive Christians understand the sense of Jesus's prayer, "Thy kingdom come, thy will be done, on earth as it is in heaven."

There's a sense of controlled urgency to this project. Reflexive spiritualists get excited about the promise and possibilities they see and the deeper truths they sense. Their excitement isn't an out-of-control zealotry, but rather a sense of groundedness and centeredness. Enthusiastic reflexive spiritualists come across as centered in a sense of having found something brilliant and resonant and so significant that it *must* be spoken. They seem to patiently insist on speaking the truth that they have found, in the face of a society that sometimes seems to them to be willfully deaf. They convey a sense of revolution and revelation, of radical perspective on essential human truths. This is the sense that comes through in the Gospel of Thomas, when Jesus says, "The Kingdom of God is spread upon the earth and *people do not see it*. If you have ears to hear, hear!" This same sense of an irritated mystic appears in the lyrics of Stuart Davis, a reflexively spiritual singer-songwriter I've quoted in other chapters: "We stifle/And smother/The mystic wonder/Is our arrogance a deafening fear/Of what we'll have to hear?"[2]

People in my field sites expressed similar feelings. Here is Cecil, speaking about the resurrection of Jesus:

> Jesus offers an invitation to a relationship that changes everything. . . .
> He invites us into a new relationship with God. . . . That Jesus arose to
> a new life, and that we can share in that new life . . . it's hard to express,
> I can't convey the impact of that new life. I have a feeling that I experi-
> ence in poetry and I only have a few pale phrases of prose to express it.

I heard the same energy coming from a First Church member when he said these words to the Faith and Reason group: "God is *in us* and *around us* and *everywhere*, *right now* and *all the time*." And in Ron's words, at Common Ground: "What is *life* fundamentally about? Experiencing the divine. Stay with that!" Author Neale Walsch spoke passionately to a five-hundred-person audience at a lecture I attended: "*We are all one*. Every religion on the face of the earth teaches that. All faiths and religions teach the unity of humankind. And yet we *can't get it!*" And in his measured, decisive tones, scholar Huston Smith told an audience, "The world's religions speak *with one voice* to the thesis that there is more to the universe than what we pick up with our senses."

The popular theology of reflexive spirituality carries the same thoughtful, intellectual tone that characterizes reflexive spirituality as a whole. But it also carries this tone of energy, determination, and inspiration. So the themes I talk about in this chapter—God's infinity, immanence, and vitalizing nature— are not just intellectual propositions that reflexive spiritualists discuss and debate. They're also about felt experience, intuition, emotion, and insight— and I hope that when you read the words of reflexive spiritualists in this chapter, you will hear this energy behind them as I did when I listened to them firsthand.

Infinite God

At one point in writing this chapter, I was considering including a Top Ten Quotes list, a list of phrases and references I heard over and over in various places throughout my fieldwork. When I put pen to paper to compose this list, it turned out to include only six items, and four of them related to the topic of this section, the concept of Infinite God. Not to put my efforts to waste, here is the annotated list of Top Four Reflexive Spirituality References Used to Point to God's Infinity:

1. "When the doors of perception are cleansed, everything will appear as it is: infinite."

This quotation from poet William Blake was very popular when I was researching this book. In my fieldwork, I heard it from Gregg Levoy, Wayne Dyer, and Common Ground's Ron and Wayne independently. I also came across it in an inspirational page-a-day calendar, an advice book for writers by Sophy Burnham, and Huston Smith's book *Why Religion Matters*.[3]

2. "Your God Is Too Small."

Your God Is Too Small is the title of a 1960 book by J.B. Phillips. Sometimes the people in my field sites referred to the book, and sometimes they appropriated the idea for themselves, as when Andrew, speaking at the Stardust, Telescopes, and God event, said, "Sometimes religions have small definitions of God."

3. "God Is a Verb."

God Is a Verb is the title of a 1998 book about mystical Judaism by David A. Cooper. Sometimes reflexive spiritualists referred to the book and sometimes just to the idea: "I like to think of God as a verb." The sense of this idea for reflexive spiritualists is that if God is a verb, not a noun, then it is something that is always happening, always unfolding, always emerging and taking shape in new ways as time goes on.

4. "And Moses asked God, 'What is your name?' And God said, 'I am that I am,' better translated as 'I will be as I will be.' You can't put God in a box; God will appear to us as God will appear."

This is the biblical story of Moses encountering God in a burning bush on Mount Horeb. It was the biblical story I heard most often during my fieldwork, and each time I heard it, it was interpreted virtually word for word as I have written it here.

Reflexive spiritualists are insistent that God should not be limited by people, that people should not be trying to put God "in a box." God, for reflexive spiritualists, is first and foremost infinite and ineffable. The transcendent transcends ordinary reality, and can't be contained in human words, human rituals, human ideas and symbols, human religions, or really anything. God can't be defined—can't be "fenced in."

This theology of God's infinity is what underlies reflexive spirituality's pluralism. If God is infinite, then no single religion can lay claim; no single religion can say, "We've got it. We know how it is about God, and we can say for sure that those other religions just don't have it right." So reflexive spiritualists take all religions as potential paths to the center, potential sources of insight about the transcendent. This theology of God's infinity also motivates reflexive spirituality's rejection of religious literalism. If God is infinite, then no set of words, no matter how divinely inspired, can completely capture it. God just can't be pinned down that way, confined to one set of expressions, stuck in one limited format.

To reflexive spiritualists, religious exclusivity—"we're right, and they're all wrong"—is sheer human arrogance in the face of divine mystery. It's the deadly sin of hubris, and that's true for literalism, too. What's more, both religious exclusivity and religious literalism seem to reflexive spiritualists like attempts to put limits on God: God can only reach you through Jesus, or through Mohammad, or through a particular religious organization, or only if you subscribe to a certain set of beliefs and practices. Reflexive spiritualists think otherwise. When they think about God in personal terms, they say that God will connect with people in whatever ways God chooses. When they use a more impersonal notion of divinity, they say that the transcendent is unlimited and a part of everything; people can connect with it anywhere.

So at First Church, David—after telling the story about Moses and the burning bush—said, "I think it's terribly, terribly presumptuous to say that God won't appear to others in other ways. God will be present in whatever ways God chooses to be present." First Church's Cecil told the Reading the Bible Intelligently class, "We can know how God has spoken to us, but we can't know that God hasn't spoken to others in other ways." Author Winifred Gallagher put it this way:

God by definition is indescribable and ineffable. . . . It's a great liberation to me to learn from rabbis that Jewishly, it's really God's business
who God is; that's what, when Moses encountered the burning bush,
he said, "Who are you," and God said, "I am who I am, Moses, it's my
business who I am, you worry about your business and I'll worry about
mine," and I think that kind of a seemly reticence about talking about
God and getting real specific about God is appropriate and reverent
and liberating.

As Gallagher suggests, a theology that emphasizes the infinite nature of
the transcendent tends to avoid "getting real specific about God." In fact, the
god of reflexive spirituality can seem pretty abstract. Even the word "God" is
sometimes too limiting—too sectarian, and too much at risk of being turned
into something literal and concrete, like an old bearded man in the sky. This
isn't so much of a problem for reflexive spiritualists in sectarian religious settings. First Church members, for example, were working within the tradition
of United Methodism, and so had no problem referring to the transcendent
as "God," though they did avoid getting any more specific than that; for example, they typically stuck to "God" and avoided "He" and "Lord."

But in nonsectarian settings, including Common Ground and the secular
settings I studied, reflexive spiritualists often ended up using very vague language to refer to the transcendent, perhaps purposefully highlighting its mysterious, infinite nature. For example, one day Ron was telling a Common
Ground class about the pluralistic view that all religions are paths to a
common center. A class participant asked him, "What's at the center?" Ron's
answer: "In the middle is the sky-blue center that is beyond articulation. Pure
presence. The mystery of the holy. What Christians call God, what in Eastern
religions is called Tao or Dharma." Jim, on another occasion, described the
transcendent as "the larger reality that enfolds us" and "the something more."

This level of abstraction has sometimes come in for criticism, not only
from people with other religious viewpoints, but also from scholars. Sociologists have sometimes interpreted an abstract notion of God as a compromise
that waters down the whole idea of divinity. Sociologists Rodney Stark and
William Sims Bainbridge, for example, have interpreted an abstract god as a
vacuous, impotent god. They once called the abstract god of reflexive spirituality "weak, vague, distant, indistinct, impersonal, and inactive" and an example of "secularized religion."[4] Their argument was that abstract concep-
tions of God actually make it *harder* for religions to offer meaning; that
religions with specific, concrete, defined images of God are more meaningful.

In their assessment, "the vague God of liberal theologians is not the God of the American people. Such a God is not behind everything that happens; one could hardly feel very close to so remote a God."[5] The only reason we have such a god at all, they believe, is because modernity brings into question more concretely defined gods. For Stark and Bainbridge, an abstract, undefinable god is a god in retreat.

My observations of reflexive spirituality in practice suggest a somewhat different way of understanding this idea of an abstract, infinite god. Stark and Bainbridge are half right: highly specific, concrete notions of God have indeed become unbelievable to many modern people. Readings between the lines of reflexive spiritualists' theological talk, it's clear that they saw themselves as having a choice of three images of God: a concrete, theistic, and unbelievable god; a believable abstract god; or no god at all. But reflexive spiritualists don't see their abstract god as a god of retreat—far from it. To them, an abstract god is a god of unlimited possibility, potency, and creative power. This is a god who, to quote David again, "will be present as God will be present—in a burning bush, in a crucified man, in a man who 'wakes up' as the Buddha did, in the human spirit, in acts of love and compassion." Or, to quote Common Ground's Ron: "This god is the initiator.... Anything and everything is possible.... This god cannot be controlled, confined, defined, conceptualized." At the Stardust, Telescopes, and God event, Simon spoke about the infinite nature of the Hebrew god, and used the same language of enormous power and vibrancy:

> When the Hebrews first started to talk about one God, they called God "sky power"—the idea was this was one god over all other gods. The sky represented the most awesome divine power.... The notion of a power we can't really identify, and it's responsible for *all this*.... They're trying to let God be as big as possible....
>
> To be moved by faith is to be moved by the incomprehensible, by mystery, by a sense of something huge beyond.... This vastness makes us feel little. Yet, we're invited to participate in what seems like a cosmic chorus, in which everything that has energy sings. We can all be part of and feel a connection that's past understanding. It's not past apprehending, obviously—we feel awe, we sense that there's mystery.... God transcends what we can think about.

With this god—an infinite, unpinned-down god—reflexive spiritualists find infinite possibilities for transcendent meaning. In scriptures, in religious traditions, in spiritual practice, and in everyday experience, there is always more than meets the eye. God gets to be everywhere, a dimension of everything that makes everything deeper, richer, and more meaningful. To reflexive spiritualists, a concrete, specific, defined god is a closed-off god, a limited and less potent god, a god that has closed the doors so that only some things—some religions, some places, some actions, some books, some people—can be possessed of transcendent meaning. With an infinite god, the possibilities for meaningfulness are infinite. For reflexive spiritualists, an infinite god is a god of infinite promise for a society suffering from the bleak meaninglessness of disenchantment.

Immanent God

The fifth item on my list of Reflexive Spirituality Pithy Sayings is the word "atonement." The significance of this word hinges on its pronunciation. Every time I heard reflexive spiritualists discuss atonement, they repeated it with two different pronunciations, like this:

5. "Atonement, at-one-ment."

By pronouncing "atonement" twice this way, reflexive spiritualists were trying to indicate what they understood the word to mean. The dictionary definition of "atonement" has to do with reparations for a crime or amends for an offense, failing, or deficiency. By this definition, atonement amounts to the payment of a fee, and it is this definition that conveys the sense of the substitutionary theory of atonement required by fundamentalist Christian theology. According to the substitutionary theory of atonement, the crucifixion of Jesus was a ransom that Jesus paid to God in exchange for God's forgiveness of the world's sins. In this interpretation, Jesus substituted for humanity in the sense that he accepted the punishment that was humanity's due.

Reflexive spiritualists find these interpretations of atonement and the crucifixion unsatisfactory. Their objections are partly theological: they find it impossible to believe in a god who would think or act that way. Their notions of God don't allow for a deity that would be that morally immature. As Cecil put it, "This is not an angry god that must be bought off." Reflexive spiritualists also have spiritual objections to the substitutionary theory of atonement: this theory simply doesn't speak to them, doesn't inspire them at all, and seems to them to offer very little by way of spiritual illumination.

Instead, reflexive spiritualists talk about "at-one-ment." By pronouncing it this way, they emphasize the potential for unity, accord, and oneness between people and the transcendent. In a state of at-one-ment, God is with us, and the specific act of at-one-ment accomplished by Jesus on the cross was an act of bringing human beings and God together existentially, as Jesus held to truth in the face of human oppression.[6] But the crucifixion of Jesus is by no means the only act of atonement that reflexive spiritualists are interested in. In the theology of reflexive spirituality, atonement in the sense of at-one-ment is about God's immanence in the world. Immanence—God dwells within the world, within people and animals and plants and the air and the water and everything. God's right here, as a First Church member said, within us and around us and everywhere, all the time. Or as Common Ground's Ron once said, it's not like there are twelve people in a room and God walks in and then there are thirteen; God's already in the room. An immanent god is not far away, but is part of everyone and everything. Everything has transcendent dimension; everything can speak to us of ultimate reality; everything is a potential revelation.

In a disenchanted world, an immanent god is a lifesaver. If God is immanent, then life and the world are not meaningless after all. On the contrary, with an immanent god, every thing, person, relationship, and action glows with transcendent significance. Ron drew on his background in religious studies to make this point: "Franz Rosenzweig said God didn't create religion, he created reality. Long before there were religions, there was already a God-saturated reality. Reality *begins* as permeated by the divine." With the concept of immanence, visions of auras, nimbuses, halos, and energy fields suddenly make poetic sense. The world is not meaningless after all; it is "crammed with heaven," as Wayne Dyer put it in a televised lecture, quoting the poet Elizabeth Barrett Browning:

> Elizabeth Barrett Browning said God is everywhere: "Earth's crammed with heaven / And every common bush afire with God / And those who truly know take off their shoes / While the rest simply sit around it and pluck blackberries." And what she's saying is when you eat a blackberry, you are seeing God in there as well.

In reflexive spirituality, God is with us, within us, within others, and in the world around us. During a talk with First Church's Faith and Reason group about the Jesus Seminar, one group member advocated for this view of God, saying:

If you look at the things the Jesus Seminar has printed in red letters, the most striking one to me is "God is in us and around us and every-where, right now and all the time." Jesus's way was exactly that. A right relationship to what's in and around us all the time is what it should be about.

For reflexive spiritualists, it is this ever-present god that makes meaning-fulness possible. On one hand, an immanent god makes life more meaningful by inspiring people to make meaning, as author Danah Zohar told a caller during a radio interview:

> With the practice of prayer, meditation, fasting, you realize that God is the creator on the outside of us, but that there is this thing inside of us that leads to asking questions, and that prayer, meditation, fasting, pondering these things of life which art, music, poetry take us to also, lead us to this thing.

Zohar is telling this caller that God is what leads people to make life mean-ingful. On the other hand, God's immanence also means that the world is al-ready meaningful, even before people take action. Common Ground's Wayne made this point:

> We have to be open to whatever the universe will tell us about the divine, because the universe is a continual revelation of the divine . . . everywhere we look is an avenue to the divine.
>
> Nature is one example. There are intrinsic meanings in nature. Nature tells a story about creation . . . birds, trees, the fragrances of nature, this is a natural revelation in process. Clouds as the earth's im-agination, and there are pictures. All of this has something to teach us about the ultimate reality or the divine.[7]

These two positions aren't contradictory for reflexive spiritualists. They go together: meaning already lives in the world, but since people are part of the world, our attentiveness is necessary to bring that meaning to light. As Common Ground's Jim said, "Everyday life is already holy, but you also make it holy by attending to it." Or, as Gregg Levoy said to participants in his Callings workshop, "Suddenly, you see all these new signs, that were there before, but now you're seeing them. To me, part of the key is *looking* for meaning."

In the theology of immanence, God is not only present in the outside world, but also in human beings. God's immanence within people gives reflexive spiritualists a sense of social and interpersonal responsibility. This is the aspect of reflexive spirituality that most lends itself to a sense of community and commitment to other people. For example, Common Ground teacher Philip Simmons, reading aloud from an essay he had written, connected God-within-me, God-within-others, and community:

> When I truly go out of myself in meeting another person, when in that encounter I can let go of my small, fearful, grasping self, then in meeting the other I simultaneously meet my own highest, truest self. If each individual being is an outflowing from—and point of access into—the same divine source that flows through all (call this source God, Life, Love, Brahman, Being, High Self, Spirit, or what you will), then in opening myself to another's essential nature, I am at the same time opening myself to my own. The biblical commandment to "love thy neighbor as thyself" is in this light transformed from a moral rule to a profound statement about the nature of relationship. I can love another only as I love myself. Conversely, I can love myself only as I love another. . . .
>
> A traditional greeting among Indian Hindus is Namaste. . . . Literally it means "I bow to you". . . . The greeting acknowledges that the other person is, like oneself, an individual manifestation of Brahman.[8]

Common Ground's Ron used the notion of God's immanence as groundwork for a sense of social responsibility:

> Does God come down and fix things, or is it an intervening through human beings? It brings up the usual question, Where was God at Auschwitz? That's the wrong question. The question is, Where was man at Auschwitz? We are the manifestations of God. We can't put it off as a separate entity to walk in the room and fix things. God acts through us.

A theology of immanence makes sense of the popular search for "meaning in everyday life" and the popularity of books about the soul. For reflexive spiritualists, this theology keeps the infinite transcendent from getting too distant. God may be abstract, but is also right here, present—closer, as the saying goes, than your own breath. A theology of immanence makes modern society meaningful by giving transcendent significance to every-one and everything. An indwelling god saturates a disenchanted world with meaningfulness.

Abundant Life: Vitalizing God

The last item on my list of Favorite Sayings of Reflexive Spiritualists is about spirit:

> 6. "Spirit comes from the Latin word for breath. Spirit is the breath of life."

For reflexive spiritualists, the transcendent breathes life into the world. The transcendent vivifies, animates, makes things come alive. Spirituality enriches people's experience of life and gives life vibrancy. Whether they call it "being in right relationship with God" or "living a mystical life" or "getting in touch with your source," reflexive spiritualists think that connecting with the tran-scendent brings new *life* into the world and allows people to more exquisitely exemplify human being.

For reflexive spiritualists, the world without the transcendent would be a world like the one Max Weber imagined: disenchanted, lifeless, and dead—what poet T.S. Eliot once called a Waste Land:

> The wind
> Crosses the brown land, unheard. The nymphs are departed.
> . . .
> We who were living are now dying
> With a little patience
> Here is no water but only rock
> . . .
> If there were the sound of water only
> Not the cicada
> And dry grass singing
> But sound of water over a rock
> Where the hermit-thrush sings in the pine trees
> Drip drop drip drop drop drop drop
> But there is no water[9]

What Eliot said in poetry, the people in my field sites said in prose. Parker Palmer, giving a public lecture, said, "Our society has limited vision. It's hard to look around and not see the many ways our society encourages death, rather than encouraging life." And Common Ground's Ron described the disenchanted world as a world without soul, a world that's all surface and no substance:

> The socialized world is largely a soulless world. We have packaged, processed foods, without much nutritional value, in contrast to being involved in producing and making a meal. The coldness of the media—the TV news, rattling off stories of death—in contrast to when the Hindenburg exploded, I remember seeing the newscaster cry.
>
> Arts have become commodities; people keep them wrapped up as an investment. Education has become about information, rather than knowledge or wisdom, which requires us to understand information in relation to life. Politics seems not to touch life. The assumption is that it's all a lie, a souped-up façade based on public opinion surveys of what people want to see and hear in the politician. It's been a long time since politics has spoken to any life issue. My students apply to grad school, and grad schools reduce the student to their GPA or their GRE score. . . .
>
> I ran across an example of the soulless the other day: There's a company that will make you a total house, a prefabricated house with all the decorating done, and they'll put up portraits of fake ancestors.

A participant at the Stardust, Telescopes, and God event used Christian language to describe the lifelessness of a world without the transcendent: "In terms of scripture, hell is the absence of God, not a place. I've known people who were living in hell. Their lives were empty. They were like the walking dead."

The walking dead is a standard symbol for a person who is living without a sense of meaning. In mythology and popular novels, this person is the zombie, the undead, going through the motions of life but spiritually dead. A modern zombie—or rather, a reluctant participant in a zombie world—is Dilbert, the comic strip engineer trapped in a technologically rational but ultimately nonsensical corporate Waste Land of his own. This corporate zombie world inspired spirituality-at-work activist Greg Pierce to say, "I like to think of us as the anti-Dilberts." At a Common Ground event on the soul, Sarah described a contemporary zombie/Dilbert she had met:

SARAH: I had a client who was soulless. He was the president of a savings and loan, and he had no capacity for understanding right and wrong. He had created havoc of his life, and he couldn't appreciate the havoc in his family. He had no passion, he never felt angry, or joy. He was blank. There were no highs and lows. He could offer a rationalization for his actions, others should accept that, and it should be okay. He was a poster child for too much corporate culture.

JIM: Don't you just know that this guy does not get art, and never taps his foot to music?

For reflexive spiritualists, spirituality—a connection to the transcendent—is the cure for the zombie life. Jeff, a participant in one of Jack Shea's discussions with business workers, applied this idea to the corporate world:

I once looked up "spirit," and of course it comes from "espiritu," which means breath, or life. Some people are talking about organizations as living systems, rather than as machines. Spirit at work, we need to see work organizations as different from a machine. If it's a machine, we don't need breath, life. If it's a living system, it needs life.

Jeff is saying that spirituality is what breathes life not only into individuals, but also into organizations. For Jeff and other reflexive spiritualists, this connection to the transcendent, to the spirit of life, is what enables people to live up to their highest potential. Wayne Teasdale, at Common Ground, called this "becoming an exquisite human being." David, at First Church, called it "expanding beyond where we went before." Author Wayne Dyer called it "finding you're a greater person than you realized." Common Ground's Ron used this idea to interpret the Christian concept of judgment:

Judgment is the realization of the extent to which you became the person you were called to be. We see this in "God calls you by your true name." All of us are called to completeness as human beings. We all want to be who we are as human beings. We want happiness, we want abundant life. . . . Being human is something we have to work at.

Ron brings up the idea that spiritual life is an answer to a call. This idea of a calling was the foundation of Gregg Levoy's Callings workshop (as well as his book by the same name). Levoy spoke about what it means to live your life in answer to a felt calling. He talked about this way of living as being spiritually awake rather than asleep:

Joseph Campbell said that more important than meaning is the sense of the rapture of being alive. What brings you to that is by definition a calling. . . . The soul cares about integrity, authenticity, richness, and the design of your life. . . .

Take a step down the path, and look at the feedback life gives you. Do I feel more awake, or asleep? . . . The story of Jonah—the captain goes around and wakes Jonah up. He's the spirit of wakefulness. The archetype of the awakener, the part of us that never went to sleep, and that's capable of waking up still.

For Levoy, the spiritual call is a call to an enhanced experience of life—a richer, more vibrant, fuller life. For David, speaking in a Christian setting, this call, this fuller life, is the work of the Holy Spirit:

Through the Holy Spirit, the routine becomes exciting, the powerless becomes empowered. The Holy Spirit brings to life and existence a dynamism. . . . Paul, in his letter to the Galatians, talked about the "fruit of the spirit." When you experience your life as love, joy, peace, gentleness, forgiveness, and self-control, you are experiencing God's spirit. If you experience life as harsh, if you are cynical or depressed, probably the spirit of God is not there at that moment.

The fifty-first psalm says, "Create in me a new heart and renew your spirit within me". . . . When God comes to the party, the fun takes on a whole new meaning and direction and purpose and power. . . . If we are open, we'll experience life as we have never experienced it before.

Excitement, dynamism, meaning, direction, purpose, power, and a renewed experience of life—this is what spiritual life is about for reflexive spiritualists. This is the "stuff" of spiritual life, this is what transcendent meaning gives to life, and this is why people bother with a spiritual life at all.

In a radio interview, Rabbi Alan Lew spoke this way about Zen meditation:

The first short-range effect is that your breath and your body become more vibrant, you become more conscious of them, and little by little, you find that you're walking around in a more vibrant world, in a world that you're more acutely conscious of, and it's a sacred world, a radiant world, all of a sudden. . . . Zen brought me into a more immediate sense of the presence of God than I had ever had before.

And at Common Ground, the ever-eloquent Ron packed the theology of abundant life and the entirety of reflexive spirituality into a few sentences in answer to a student's question at the end of a class:

ANDREW: Spirituality: what is it?
RON: That abundant life to which all the traditions say we are called. Joy, bliss, the full activation of the chakras, whatever trope you want to use. And what's the beginning of the path to that abundant life? Receptivity. Attention. Paying attention. Catching ourselves when we're being reactive, and being creative instead. What is spirituality? It's who we are. And who we are at our deepest level is the divine reality. And getting to that level is spirituality. And how do we begin? Attention and receptivity.

Abundant life is really the ultimate sense of reflexive spirituality; it's what everything else is aimed at producing. The value of the transcendent is its capacity to enliven everything it touches. The reason to have a spiritual life is to have more of a life in general—a deeper life, a richer life; the experience, as Joseph Campbell said, of being alive. And the reason to have a spiritual culture, one that talks about ultimate values and meanings, is to bring renewed vitality to modern society—to make wisdom and insight our social currency, to render us more creative as a society, and to enchant a disenchanted world.

An infinite, immanent, vitalizing god is a god tailor-made for a disenchanted society. An infinite god makes for infinite possibilities for meaning: there are no limits; new meaning is always possible; and God can speak to people in many, many ways. An immanent god brings that meaningful potential into everyday life—everything is a potential revelation, everyone is a window into divinity, and everything and everyone is connected. And into a flat, gray, deadened world, a vitalizing god brings abundant life—spirit, energy, creativity, possibility, breath.

This theology is built using tools of intellectual rationality. It's modern through and through. But it also absolutely affirms the reality and significance of the transcendent. God is not dead, reflexive spiritualists are saying, but it might not be the god you thought you knew.[10] This god, this theology, is the child of a union between the modern tradition of intellectual rationality and the religious tradition of transcendent reality. In a reflexive modernity, we are continually making revisions based on new knowledge and ideas.[11] A reflexive spirituality introduces the possibility that some of those revisions might be about reincorporating transcendent meaning into modern life.

7 YOU CAN'T PUT REFLEXIVE SPIRITUALITY IN A BOX

Most of this book is about the core themes of reflexive spirituality—the kinds of spiritual talk that I heard repeatedly in different field sites. At its core, reflexive spirituality is about people pursuing meaning through a creative interplay between rationality and spirituality. Chapters 3 through 6 describe different aspects of this creative interplay: How do reflexive spiritualists use spiritual wisdom to point out the limitations of strict rationalism? How do they use reason to get spiritual meaning from religious traditions? How do the spiritual insights they arrive at speak to the problem of meaning in modern society? The way reflexive spiritualists answered these questions were similar in my different field sites. In a variety of different contexts, reflexive spiritualists had similar ways of "getting a spirituality that makes sense."

But reflexive spirituality is a broad, organically emerging cultural sensibility, not an authoritative doctrine that's meant to be exactly the same everywhere. And so it can look a little different everywhere. I spent most of my research time in three different kinds of settings: a large Protestant church, an interfaith education center, and a variety of secular settings where people were talking about spirituality. These different settings all focused on different things, and their different focuses colored their spiritual talk. The members of First United Methodist Church, for example, used reflexive spirituality to relate to one primary religious tradition: Christianity. Common Grounders were exploring a variety of religious traditions to gain wisdom. In secular settings, people used reflexive spirituality to shore up their sense that spiritual meaning is still possible even in a skeptical secular society.

These settings all have their own history, traditions, and preoccupations, even as they share a broader value for spiritual meaning. Their differences led them to emphasize different things, to use reflexive spirituality for slightly different purposes and in slightly different ways. This chapter talks about each of my three field sites one by one so that you can see some of the ways that reflexive spirituality takes shape in different settings with unique purposes. At the end of the chapter, I draw on other studies and anecdotal data to give my impressions of how reflexive spirituality might take shape differently in settings that I haven't studied systematically.

Reflexive Christianity: First United Methodist Church

First United Methodist Church was firmly grounded in the Protestant tradition of United Methodism. Members used a Christian vocabulary and talked a lot about Jesus. Their reflexive spirituality was a reflexive Christianity. In general, reflexive spiritualists are aiming for a spirituality that makes sense and still speaks to them of transcendent meaning. First Church's reflexive Christians were aiming for a Christianity that would make sense, offer meaning, and feel true to the spirit of Christianity.

The reflexive spiritualists at First Church saw themselves as in a debate with Protestant fundamentalism. Chapter 2 described the longstanding differences between liberal and conservative Christianity, and this ongoing conflict created a context that influenced First Church members' reflexive spirituality. For example, as Chapter 3 explained, reflexive spiritualists in all my settings criticized cultural patterns associated with technological rationality. But at First Church, these criticisms took on a particular cast, because members strongly associated technological rationality with religious fundamentalism. First Church members saw fundamentalists as caught up in the patterns of technological rationality. From their point of view, fundamentalists are using technological rationality to relate to religious tradition, and that's causing all kinds of problems.

So while reflexive spiritualists in general disliked overly literalistic approaches to life, First Church members were especially critical of Biblical literalism. Reflexive spiritualists in general criticized an overreliance on rules and routine, but First Church members were especially frustrated by attempts to reduce Christianity to a set of behavioral rules—"quid pro quo Christianity," as one member called it. And reflexive spiritualists in all my settings warned against what I've called "closure," but First Church members were especially critical of attempts to treat Christianity as a set of definitive "answers to life." First Church members also criticized scientism—they certainly believed that purely materialistic approaches to life were missing something—but this wasn't a point of debate with fundamentalist Christians, so they didn't talk about it as much or as forcefully as they talked about the other three dimensions of technological reason.

First Church members' debate with Protestant fundamentalism led them to strongly emphasize metaphorical interpretation of the Bible; sermons and discussion groups spent a lot of time talking about different ways of interpreting Biblical stories and sayings. And even aside from the debate with fundamentalism, just being a Protestant church influenced First Church's practice of reflexivity, pluralism, and mysticism. For example, the Protestant traditions of weekly sermons and Sunday School offered the congregation a variety of contexts to promote reflexivity, which they did a lot. Reflexivity was a central group project at First Church—David and Joan promoted it from the pulpit, and a variety of adult Sunday School classes and discussion groups gave churchgoers regular opportunities to reflect together on the different possible meanings of Christian symbols, stories, and rituals.

First Church members were focused on the project of reflexively renewing Christianity—"getting a Christianity that speaks to us where we live." So while they advocated pluralism in the broad sense of "all religions are valid paths to God," they spent less time talking about other religious traditions than people in my other field sites did. When they did study other religions and other religious leaders, part of their purpose was to illuminate their Christianity. One member found, for example, that Mahatma Gandhi helped him understand what it meant to "live as Christ." Other members found that stories about the Buddha helped them reflect on the teachings of Jesus. In their studies of other religions, some members found a refreshing emphasis on spiritual practice over religious belief. They were inspired to incorporate consistent spiritual practices such as prayer and meditation into their own lives, and felt that this had deepened their relationship with God. And other members found that the study of different religions reinforced Christian teachings: one member of Cecil's Religions of the World class said, "I'm struck by what I increasingly see as the commonalities in all our religions. . . . The Buddhist definition of grace is one of the best descriptions of grace I've seen."

First Church's Protestant heritage also influenced how members talked about mysticism. Compared with some religious traditions, mainline Protestants have often downplayed mysticism, but it does appear in talk about the Holy Spirit and "experiencing God's presence." When members spoke about experiencing God's presence, it was usually in the context of a discussion about how to interpret Christian doctrine. A member of the Faith and Reason group, for example, said, "I accept God, I have satisfying experiences of God's presence.... The triune God is not important to me. It's somewhere round or in me, and that's good enough for me." The word "mysticism" itself came up mostly in the Faith and Reason group, during discussions of "ways of knowing God." There were several women in this group who regularly brought up mysticism as a legitimate way of knowing God; others in the group generally agreed and then moved on. So mysticism had its place at First Church, in the general sense of valuing the experience of God over adherence to doctrine, but as a group, First Church members didn't talk about mysticism as much as people in my other field sites did.

First Church's commitment to Christianity of course affected its theology. In contrast to my other, nonsectarian field sites, its theology was very Jesus-centric; members spent a lot of time talking about what Jesus said and did, as well as the theological status of Jesus. They emphasized Jesus as a way-shower, a guide along the spiritual path. In other words, Jesus was most important to First Church members as the person who best helped them find God and live in the world—rather than, for example, the person who paid for humanity's sins by dying on the cross, or one third of the divine trinity. Members' conversations about Jesus were filled with lines like these:

> Jesus is the one who, for me, leads me to my best understanding of God ... and is the model of authentic living.

> Jesus is not the solution—Jesus is the problem. Jesus brought turmoil and confusion to how we understand the divine. He's not a peaceful source of harmony, but rather that which makes us think about life, and challenges the order of the day.

> Jesus challenged the way things are stacked.... He said, "There is a new way ... Turn around, and act in a new way, according to a new principle."

And these words from David in a sermon:

> Jesus was obedient to God's will. Obedient to death. . . . Jesus was faithful to God and committed in love to other human beings. He

lived that pattern. He was killed in the line of holy duty, because he
lived that pattern of life. His life is an invitation for you and me to live
that pattern as well. . . . It's a way of life that Jesus commends to us: Your
will be done, not mine.

Sometimes, First Church members talked about Jesus as the image of
God, and discussed what image of God he offered. One member, for example,
said, "Jesus is supposed to be our best image of God, and the Bible depicts
Jesus as a sufferer, not as a sender of lightning bolts and almighty." Most often,
though, First Church members looked to Jesus as the model of piety, of what
it means to live a life in obedience to God.

First Church members shared with other reflexive spiritualists the core
themes described in earlier chapters: they criticized technological reason; embraced reflexivity, metaphor, pluralism, and mysticism; and valued an infinite,
immanent, life-giving God. But their reflexive spirituality was specifically a
reflexive Christianity. They used reflexive spirituality to revitalize Christianity, to articulate some of their disagreements with conservative Christianity,
and to consider what it means to be a follower of Jesus.

Spirituality: Searching for Meaning in Secular Life

First United Methodist Church was a Christian institution and so was
wrapped in the context of a particular religious tradition. The secular settings
I observed were not engaged with any particular religious tradition—but they
were still dealing with tradition. My secular field sites were wrapped in the
context of secular America and its tradition of technological reason. So where
First Church members were trying to revitalize Christianity and get a Christianity that made sense to them, reflexive spiritualists in my secular field sites
were trying to revitalize secular culture and get a secular life that inspired
them. In both settings, the goal was meaning—a meaningful Christianity or
a meaningful secularity.

First Church members were operating in a religious context and so could
take some religious ideas for granted. The idea of God, for example—anyone
who found the idea of God unbelievable probably wouldn't belong to a mainline Protestant church. In secular settings, things were different. Reflexive
spiritualists couldn't take for granted that the people they were talking to
were even willing to entertain the possibility that a transcendent or spiritual
reality might exist. The idea of a transcendent context within which life might
be interpreted inspires ridicule in some sections of secular society, indiffer-
ence in others, and rage in still others. My secular field sites, then, were facing

the disenchanted world head on. This was especially true of the Spirit-at-Work movement. These business people saw the corporate world that they were coming from as "especially secular"—concerned exclusively with material realities and dominated by a here-and-now, practical, utilitarian logic.

In secular settings, and especially in the spirit-at-work movement, reflexive spiritualists were very conscious of how powerful technological rationality is. They called it by different names—"the business world" or "modern society" or "the culture"—but they described it in terms of the same four patterns I talked about in Chapter 3: literalism, scientism, rules and routine, and closure. They felt these patterns to be overwhelming in the business world and in society in general. They were especially critical of scientism—the kind of practical materialism that assumes that all there is and all that matters is what we can know using our five senses. To even talk about spirituality, reflexive spiritualists in secular settings seemed to have to engage in constant refrains of "There's more than meets the eye."

On the other hand, because they weren't wrapped up in an intrareligious dialogue about scriptural interpretation, reflexive spiritualists in secular settings didn't spend as much time criticizing Biblical literalism as First Church members did. But they did criticize literalism more broadly: they often talked about how limiting it is to insist on "one right way" or "one true meaning" or "one correct interpretation" of life's events. They pointed out the limits of relying too much on rules and routines when they criticized bureaucratic "red tape" and meaningless policies and procedures in general. And they were vocal critics of premature closure: they criticized American society, and the business world in particular, for focusing on answers, goals, and results to a degree that made it next to impossible to be truly creative and attentive.

When it came to spirituality and religious tradition, reflexive spiritualists in secular settings took pluralism to an extreme. While First Church members used pluralism to enhance their Christianity, reflexive spiritualists in secular settings used it to line up an arsenal to fight rampant disenchantment. They wanted to gather together every religious tradition; every historical period; and every poet, philosopher, artist, writer, and leader to say (in my words, not theirs), "Look! *All of these* say that there's *something more*. Doesn't that make you think that it just might possibly be true?" So it was in secular settings that I most often heard people refer to "religious traditions" or "spiritual traditions" or "wisdom traditions" as one collective entity, speaking with one voice against a secular vision of reality. As the ever-cogent Huston Smith put it in a public lecture, "The world's religions speak *with one voice* to the thesis that there is more than the physical universe we pick up with our senses."

Mysticism, for reflexive spiritualists in secular settings, was about experiencing the transcendent, and the way to cultivate that experience was through some kind of regular practice that would keep people in touch with spiritual realities: meditating, praying, journaling, reading spiritual or religious books, participating in discussion groups, working with a spiritual mentor or coach, or going on spiritual retreats. Metaphorical interpretation of scriptures wasn't a front-line issue in secular settings, but metaphorical interpretation of life was. People often looked for the metaphorical significance of life events, looking for the transcendent meanings that these events might, upon reflection, disclose.[1] And reflexivity was about committing to ongoing inquiry about the transcendent and regularly reflecting on the role of the transcendent in one's own life. Authors and public speakers often described religious and philosophical study as part of their own reflexive process.

The most urgent theological problem in secular settings was resuscitating transcendent meaning. Because technological rationality is an equal-opportunity destroyer of transcendent meaning in all kinds of religions as well as in secular life, reflexive spiritualists in secular settings wanted, first and foremost, to open a space for spirituality to be possible at all. So when they talked theology, they spent a lot of time making the case that some kind of transcendent truth—whether we think of it as God or divinity or ultimate reality—is actually real and important, and not a ludicrous or irrelevant idea. Their main message was first, that the transcendent exists at all, and second, that it matters. The specifics of that message got less attention in these settings than in the other settings I studied.

One way of understanding this commitment to generality is by seeing reflexive spiritualists in secular settings as the front line of an effort to rescue some sense of transcendent reality for a skeptical society. In that kind of situation, the fine points of theology just aren't what matters most. What matters most is hammering home the fundamental message: "There's something more, and that matters." So in secular settings, reflexive spiritualists spoke in the broadest terms possible to convey this message without any sectarian nitpicking. Author Danah Zohar, for example, told listeners about studies that suggest that surgery patients who have "a belief system or a deep sense of purpose or meaning in their lives actually heal faster than the patients who don't have this deep sense of meaning or purpose." She used similar words to describe Victor Frankl's theory of concentration camp victims' psychology:

> Frankl's basic insight was that those people who survived the concentration camps were the people who did believe in something or had

some deep sense of purpose, something to carry them through, that they wanted to live for when they got out of the camps. Whereas those prisoners who didn't particularly believe in anything, didn't have any deep sense of purpose or value, just simply couldn't cope with the horrors of the camps, and they died.

Zohar is using the most general terms possible to argue that transcendent meaning of some kind—any kind—does matter. Author Winifred Gallagher spoke in equally general terms to make a similar point about how the transcendent can bring meaning to suffering. Her college-age son was diagnosed with cancer, and in the subsequent months and years, she found that she "had actually come to trust in *some great good thing at the center of being*, that in some inconceivable way was going to make this make sense at some point in the inconceivable future. And that's what really made me realize that I had become a religious person." Wayne Dyer drew on Aldous Huxley's theory of the perennial philosophy to make the same general points:

> The perennial philosophy. Aldous Huxley looked at wisdom, religion, philosophies from all over in time and space. . . . One, there is a world beyond the world of the changing. . . . Two, we are connected to that never-changing world. . . . And it's almost as if we have to begin to know that world.

Reflexive spiritualists in secular settings are engaged in a kind of "Transcendence 101." They see a society wrapped up in a kind of here-and-now expediency—a society where the cool kids are all smirking, wise-to-the-scene skeptics who aren't going to let anyone pull the wool over their eyes about some kind of "transcendence" nonsense. And they see this kind of society as a spiritual straitjacket. So over and over, reflexive spiritualists found creative ways to hammer home the basic message that spirituality is valid and important, even though modern life makes it difficult to make sense of.

Finding Wisdom in the World's Religions: Interfaith Spirituality at Common Ground

Common Ground was an interfaith educational center, and these two themes—interfaith and education—guided its practice of reflexive spirituality. As an interfaith organization, Common Ground was in between the religious setting of First Church and the secular settings I observed. On one hand, Common Grounders faced many of the same issues that First Church members faced, but in reference to all religions and not just Christianity. So where First Church argued with Christian fundamentalism, Common Grounders argued with fundamentalism in general. First Church members spent time reinterpreting traditional Christian symbols; Common Grounders spent time reinterpreting symbols of the world's religions in general. On the other hand, Common Ground is not religiously affiliated—it's an adult education center—so members couldn't take any particular religious vocabulary for granted, as First Church members could. And like the people in the secular settings I studied, Common Grounders engaged a lot with secular images of reality. Common Grounders were vocal in their criticisms of the different limitations of technological rationality, and they were eloquent in their advocacy and use of metaphor, pluralism, reflexivity, and mysticism in the pursuit of transcendent meaning.

What most distinguished Common Ground from my other field sites was its emphasis on all religions as sources of wisdom. For Common Grounders, all religions offer guidance about how human beings can relate to the transcendent, and the world's religions are a treasure trove of meaning, wisdom, and spiritual insight. Their goal was wisdom and connection with the transcendent, and they saw themselves as mining the world's religions to gain more and more insight about how to meaningfully relate to the transcendent, other people, and the world.

So when Common Grounders criticized forms of religiosity that focus heavily on rules, their logic was that "just following the rules" doesn't promote wisdom or meaningful relationship with the transcendent. From their point of view, God is way more than just a rule-giver, and to emphasize rules is to remain a spiritual toddler. They wanted people to learn to relate to the "ground of being" in a richer, more grown-up, sophisticated way. Likewise, Common Grounders' criticisms of literalism and closure were elaborate critiques of narrowness of vision. "If you want rich meaningfulness," they seemed to be saying, "you have to be open to more than one possibility; you have to be open to change and evolution."

Pluralism was central to this interfaith organization. They talked about it directly, and often used the word "pluralism" itself. Pluralism made sense for Common Grounders as an approach to religious diversity that offers up more possible insight than religious inclusivism, exclusivism, or relativism.[2] If religions are all archives of wisdom and resources for meaning—and that's how Common Grounders saw it—then it just doesn't make sense to discount any of them a priori or to decide up front that their insights are only of limited validity. Instead, Common Ground's leaders encouraged their students to approach all religions as potential sources of meaning, wisdom, and insight, even as they delved deeply into or identified with one or two particular traditions.

Common Ground's pluralism led to a very developed sense of mysticism. Teachers strongly emphasized mysticism as the central place where all religions come together. They taught a mystical theology that drew on the published works and journals of mystics throughout history. They consistently promoted meditation, and they were eloquent about the difference between the discipline of a mystical life and what Ron called "spiritual masturbation"— by which he meant a more casual (and, as he saw it, self-indulgent) approach to spirituality that consisted of occasional "spiritual highs" at weekend retreats and similar activities.

Because Common Ground is an interfaith organization, it was consciously operating against the backdrop of past and present conflict between religious groups. Common Grounders were very aware of the reality of interreligious conflict and violence, and they wanted to promote interreligious understanding and dialogue instead. They were aware, too, that many nonreligious people have negative feelings about religion because they associate it with conflict and violence.

This backdrop not only added force to Common Grounders' pluralism; it also influenced the popular theology they promoted. Like reflexive spiritualists in my other field sites, Common Grounders talked about the infinite, immanent, and vitalizing nature of the divine. But they also talked about the *unitive* nature of the transcendent: God's oneness. Common Grounders' particular attention to pluralism, mysticism, and interreligious understanding all dovetailed in a theology of unity. In this theology, God unites all people by uniting each person with God. Indeed, in their panentheistic theology, God is all there is, and the whole of creation is a part or manifestation of God. There is only one, and we are all part of that one. This message of oneness was important to Common Grounders; their classes were filled with statements like these:

> The goal of a mystical life is always about union or integration with ultimate reality.

> The essence of reality is an all-encompassing unity that generates and embraces diversity. . . . We're not creatures fashioned by God; we're temporary manifestations of God, though certainly not the totality of God.

Mystics have a profound sense of connectedness with everyone and everything. Individual projects for happiness are illusory if they don't take into account the happiness of everyone and everything else.

If—as Buddhists, Hindus, Jains, Taoists, [and others] say—our separateness from others is illusion, then others' spiritual fulfillment matters.

Reflexive spiritualists in my different field sites often seemed to me to be speaking to absent others. At First Church, those absent others were conservative Christians. In secular settings, the absent others were either religious skeptics or people who just took a scientistic, materialistic view of the world for granted and never thought much about spiritual realities. Common Grounders were speaking to all those groups, and they were also speaking to everyone who thinks that for one religion to be true, the others have to be false or "less true." Against a backdrop of "one right way" and "one best way" approaches to religion, Common Grounders spoke about the wisdom that we can gain if we're open to considering multiple religious perspectives. And in the context of interreligious conflict, they spoke about oneness, arguing that people are all united with God and one another.

Reflexive Catholicism: Negotiating with Magisterial Authority

Scholars Jerome Baggett and Michele Dillon have each published books that talk about reflexivity among Catholics. These books aren't specifically about reflexive *spirituality*, but *reflexivity* more broadly is a prominent theme in both. Dillon's book *Catholic Identity: Balancing Reason, Faith, and Power* is a study of pro-change Catholics. The kind of change Dillon focuses on is social change, in contrast to the more theological change that I focus on in this book. So the reflexive Catholicism that she describes is a moral reflexivity more than a spiritual reflexivity—not that these aren't intertwined. But while I (and the people I studied) talk a lot about transcendent meaning, wisdom, and spiritual insight, Dillon's book—and the people the book is about—talk about creating spaces for gay and lesbian Catholics, advocating for the ordination of women as priests, and challenging the church's prohibition of abortion.

There is certainly a relationship between spirituality and social activism within the church. For example, Dillon shows how pro-change Catholics used doctrine to critique doctrine, in a classic reflexive pattern: they identified some aspects of doctrine—for example, justice—as fundamental, and criticized practices of discrimination as conflicting with these fundamental principles. At the same time, because of Dillon's focus on social issues, it's hard to get a good sense of how the Catholics she studied might use their reflexivity in relation to specifically theological questions. But a few things are clear: pro-change Catholics believe that it's valid for people to interpret doctrines, scriptures, and sacraments differently. They innovate, creating new ways of being Catholic, while retaining a strong identification with Catholic tradition. They temper the idea of complete obedience to church authority: they believe that people must use their consciences and their capacity for reason in combination with church doctrine to arrive at their own conclusions. As Dillon puts it, despite the Vatican's claim to interpretive authority, pro-change Catholics have a more democratic understanding of Catholicism; they locate interpretive authority in the everyday activities of ordinary Catholics.[3] Above all, Dillon emphasizes that pro-change Catholics believe in the fruitful combination of faith and reason in the pursuit of moral righteousness.

Jerome Baggett's book *Sense of the Faithful: How American Catholics Live Their Faith* is about Catholicism more broadly. He describes how Catholics reflexively engage the church's stance on social and moral issues, but also how they reflexively engage more theological matters like the kinds of things I discuss in this book. For example, most of the Catholics that Baggett spoke with believed (consistent with church teaching) that Bible stories are symbolic and not meant to be taken literally. They were self-aware about their own interpretive process—they knew, for example, that they were constructing different images of God, and they were careful about which image they were invoking at particular times. Many of them described a complex, inscrutable God, and Baggett even quotes one church member as saying that people sometimes "put God in a box" and that God "doesn't even come close to fitting in that box."[4]

Some built on this sense of God's inscrutability to embrace religious pluralism: "I think . . . God is so great and so unfathomable that there are going to be different ways for each of us to draw near to God,"[5] though others maintained (again, consistent with church teachings) the inclusivist stance that Catholicism contains more of the truth than other religions do.[6] Like First Church members, the Catholics that Baggett spoke with often made "not" statements about God that marked their disagreement with technologically rational images of God: "God isn't up there with a scorecard deciding who wins and who loses." "I don't think God's an accountant keeping track of every little thing people do."[7] Finally, many of the Catholics that Baggett spoke with had a reflexive relationship to church authority, questioning the value of the hierarchy, placing primacy on personal conscience, criticizing the church for sometimes being in conflict with the example of Jesus, and sometimes explicitly comparing the church (negatively) to a corporation.[8] These examples, and Baggett's own analysis, suggest that a reflexive spirituality something like I describe in this book is alive and well among American Catholics.

But American Catholicism is a unique context, just as the Protestant First United Methodist Church and the interfaith Common Ground were unique contexts. How does a Catholic reflexive spirituality look different from reflexive spirituality in these other settings? In a nutshell, what I see in the reflexive Catholicism that Baggett describes is the influence of the powerful Catholic magisterium. Reflexive Catholics seem to be operating against a historical backdrop in which it was important to be a "good Catholic" and in which good Catholics obeyed magisterial authority and adhered to the doctrines, edicts, beliefs, and pronouncements of the Vatican. This history and this authority structure have been so powerful that reflexive Catholics are occupied by redefining what it means to be "a good Catholic." For example, one of the people Baggett interviewed said, "Being a good Catholic is about choosing to follow Jesus through the church but not letting the church corrupt your faith,"[9] and another said:

> I would say that being a good Catholic in the traditional sense is going to Mass regularly, giving your time and money to the church, praying regularly, and embodying the beliefs of the Catholic religion in how you treat other people. I try to do that stuff. Overall, though. . . . since I don't know many of the fundamental doctrines of the religion, I mostly do this by trying to be a good person.[10]

By contrast, I never heard First Church members talk about what it means to be "a good United Methodist"—or even "a good Christian." They did sometimes say things like "I don't have to believe that Jesus was literally born of a virgin to be a Christian"—but they were arguing against the fundamentalist notion of correct beliefs, not against a notion of obedience to church authority.

To my (non-Catholic) mind, the language of "a good Catholic" brings up images of children relating to their parents. And indeed, Baggett makes this analogy explicit when he quotes psychologist Eugene Kennedy's words about American Catholicism: "To act independently and responsibly cannot always be accurately depicted as a revolt against authority. Most people regard it as growing up."[11] Baggett's analysis also reflects the parent-like power of the magisterium: he describes reflexive Catholics as "negotiating" with their tradition. In fact, this idea of negotiation is central to his conceptualization of reflexive Catholicism. In his analysis, reflexive spirituality among American Catholics is about individual Catholics reflecting on official doctrine in light of their own experiences and deciding which aspects of official doctrine to adopt for themselves and which ones to reject or to regard as less important. Adolescents go through a similar process as they gradually separate from their parents and decide which of their parents' opinions, attitudes, and priorities to take on for themselves, which to reject, and which to simply play down.

This sense of reflexive spirituality as an ongoing negotiation with authority was not so strong in my field sites—except perhaps among the Spirit-at-Work people, who were also engaged with a very powerful bureaucracy, although the corporate world operates with more anonymous leadership. First Church members, though, as well as Common Grounders, seemed to take their own authority for granted. First Church members gave a much stronger sense of their tradition being a democracy. And so they talked over and over about how to "get a Christianity that speaks to us where we live" and "create a Christianity that works for the twenty-first century" and "get a Christianity that makes sense in a postmodern world." As a result, their reflexivity didn't take on a tone of negotiating an individual identity in relation to a powerful authority. Instead, it took on a tone more akin to spiritual activism.

Judging from Baggett's work in particular, reflexive spirituality among American Catholics seems to share core themes with reflexive spirituality in other settings. But just as in other settings, Catholic reflexive spiritualists are dealing with their own unique set of historical and institutional circumstances, and their practice of reflexive spirituality reflects those unique circumstances. In particular, the Catholic Church's powerful bureaucratic authority structure seems to give reflexive Catholicism a "negotiating" quality, and the church's vocal, conservative stance on various social and moral issues may make these issues more prominent in the reflexive work of Catholics than they are for other reflexive spiritualists.

Hints of a Reflexive Judaism

I only have anecdotal evidence about reflexive spirituality among American Jews. I want to describe three such anecdotes that might give some sense of the flavor of reflexive Judaism. A systematic study would tell us much more.

- Common Grounders often have classes built around particular books. During my research, one of these books was *Minyan: Ten Principles for Living a Life of Integrity*, written by Rabbi Rami Shapiro. In the book's preface, Shapiro writes:

> Certainly Judaism is filled with doing, but the doings to which I was exposed as a child were rituals performed without real purpose or understanding. My family observed the holy days and Shabbat (Sabbath), because we were commanded to do so. Fulfilling our obligations to God and tradition seemed to be the whole of Judaism. One was a good Jew if one conformed to the ways of the old Jews. I wanted something more. . . . I wanted a Jewish spiritual practice that would infuse my days with light, with joy, with peace, with a transcendent sense of meaning and purpose. . . . My goal was to create a center for a nondenominational, post-Halachic Judaism that used tradition and Hasidic teaching as vehicles for deepening spiritual awareness. . . .
>
> Minyan is a path of daily spiritual living based on ten *hanhagot*, spiritual disciplines, which have been practiced by Jews for centuries. Minyan is not a substitute for Jewish tradition. You practice Minyan in addition to everything else you do as a Jew. . . . Minyan has one aim: to awaken you to God as the source and substance of reality.[12]

With *Minyan*, Shapiro seems to be doing with Jewish ritual something like what First Church members were doing with Christian scripture. Both seem to have a sense that their tradition has devolved into simple, rote traditionalism and so has lost meaningfulness. And both are reaching back into their tradition for alternatives to renew their spiritual lives.

During a Common Ground discussion of *Minyan*, Ron read to the class a column that Shapiro had recently published in the *Miami Herald*. Shapiro wrote of the "mystical core" that all religions share and announced his intention to start a center designed to "help people realize this common ground, so that we can recognize our differences while realizing our commonalities. We are, as human beings, all heirs to all the world's religious traditions."[13]

- ALEPH, the Alliance for Jewish Renewal, lists eighteen foundational principles on its Web site. Among them are these:

> "What/whom the traditions experienced as transcendent God we meditate on and worship in ways that honor both the tradition and our intuition as to how we are addressed by that God in the present."

"We see the human spirit and the Divine as one evolving process that calls upon us all for the interaction we call Godwrestling ('Yisrael') and 'Gathering the Sparks.'"

"In the sacred texts of the Jewish people and the writings of Jewish spiritual teachers of previous generations we find enormous wisdom and insight that draw on Eternal truth and continue to have great potential to aid human beings in their quest for personal growth, empowerment, and healing—as well as those elements that are historically limited and need to be transcended. We will study, teach, and make accessible these texts and writings with all those who wish to encounter them, wrestle with their content and meaning, and decide what to draw on and what to leave behind."

"We are committed to consult with other spiritual traditions, sharing with them what we have found in our concerned research and trying out what we have learned from them, to see whether it enhances the special truths of the Jewish path."

"We are committed to applying all of these values and principles to the renewal and revitalization of our personal and communal ceremonies, liturgies, rituals, life-paths, and spiritual practices, and to our processes for collective decisions-making and collective actions."[14]

- The Jewish Reconstructionist Federation (JRF) has an essay entitled "Is Reconstructionist Judaism for You?" on its website. According to this essay, "Reconstructionist Judaism is a progressive, contemporary approach to Jewish life which integrates a deep respect for traditional Judaism with the insights and ideas of contemporary social, intellectual and spiritual life." The essay continues:

"Torah" means "teaching." In Jewish tradition, Talmud Torah, the study of Torah, is a life-long obligation and opportunity. Reconstructionists are committed to a serious engagement with the texts and teachings, as well as the art, literature and music of tradition. But we are not passive recipients; we are instead challenged to enter the conversation of the generations and to hear voices other than our own, but to add our own voices as well.[15]

Shapiro, ALEPH, and the JRF voice themes similar to those I heard in my field sites: reflexive engagement with one's own tradition, pluralistic engagement with other traditions, interest in mysticism as a point of intersection among religions, and the desire to renew tradition, rather than rejecting it or granting it ultimate authority. It's not clear from these three little anecdotes just what unique qualities would characterize a Jewish reflexive spirituality—maybe, as Shapiro suggests, a reflexive Judaism would emphasize the renewal of ritual; maybe, as ALEPH and the JRF suggest, it would tap into Judaism's long tradition of study; or maybe it would be influenced by other unique aspects of Jewish tradition, Jewish history, or Jews' status in the United States and abroad.

Like God, reflexive spirituality can't be put in a box. I've defined it around several core themes that have to do with a critique of technological reason, a way of relating to religious tradition, and a popular theology. I found those themes consistently across my different field sites, and I see them pop up in others' studies of reflexive Catholics and in anecdotal observations of American Jews and the culture at large. But reflexive spirituality is really a set of tools, an approach to relating to religious tradition and creating spiritual meaning, and people can use these tools or this approach in different ways. The institutional and cultural contexts that reflexive spiritualists are involved with influence how they practice reflexive spirituality together when they're in those contexts. So on a large scale, a Protestant reflexive spirituality looks a little different from an interfaith reflexive spirituality, a secular reflexive spirituality, and probably a Catholic or Jewish reflexive spirituality. And on a smaller scale, there may be differences between how people in different United Methodist churches or different secular settings or different Jewish temples practice reflexive spirituality, and in the kinds of things that people in those settings use reflexive spirituality to do.[16]

8 CONNECTIONS

When I began researching this book, the loudest voices in the American conversation about religion were arguing that schools should teach creationism in science classes and that Christianity is the one true religion. Since then, another voice has come to sound equally loud: a collection of writers nicknamed "the new atheists" argues that religions of all kinds are irrational. They urge people to reject religion and choose reason instead.

As in politics, it is the most black-and-white, divisive, strident voices that get the most media attention. And so people with more nuanced perspectives on religion, reason, and spirituality come to feel voiceless by comparison. Or, perhaps more commonly, they just think that they're unique, and alone. Not wanting their thoughts caricatured, and not wanting to knock the chip off anyone's shoulder, they sometimes decide to just keep quiet. As a friend of mine, Colleen, tells me, when the conversation in her community turns to religion, she just says, "My ideas about religion are kind of unique" and leaves it at that. Her "unique ideas"? Different religions can be equally good sources of insight, some religious ideas are better understood metaphorically than literally, having a spiritual life is more important than having the right doctrinal beliefs, and asking good questions is more important than having "correct" answers. Sound familiar?

The truth is that Colleen is not alone. People in a variety of contexts are engaging religion and reason together to create a spiritual life that works for them intellectually. These people value metaphor more than literalism, spiritual experience more than religious doctrine, complex questions more than simple answers, and an abundance of religious traditions rather than just one or none at all. They're frustrated by narrow rationalities that get in the way of deeper meanings, and they find meaning in an infinite transcendent that is at the same time right here in the midst of things, giving daily life its vitality.

One of the main messages of this book is not for scholars, but for readers who recognize themselves in its pages. That message is: You are not alone. There is a loose subculture of people engaged with questions of meaning, spirituality, divinity, religion, and reason. This subculture exists both inside and outside of traditional religious institutions.

The scholarly message of this book is also about reason and religion, because these are the two legs that reflexive spirituality stands on. Reflexive spirituality is heir to religious traditions and to the Enlightenment tradition of systematic reason. Its central concern, meaning, is intellectual. Yet meaning is also spiritual—it's something felt, intuited, as a sense of perspective, insight, or wisdom. As a spirituality focused on the pursuit of transcendent meaning, reflexive spirituality tries to take full advantage of the meaning-making resources offered by our traditions of reason and our traditions of religion. Reflexive spiritualists use reason and religion together, putting them in dialogue with each other. They use the insights of religious traditions to critique the limitations that technological rationality places on transcendent meaning. And they use the inheritance of intellectual reason to find new meaning in religious traditions.

Can Reflexive Spirituality Bring Meaning to Modern Society? The View from Social Theory

Clearly, the people whose words appear in this book are finding personal meaning in reflexive spirituality. But what about meaning as a social problem? Can reflexive spirituality have an effect on modern culture? I've described reflexive spirituality not only as a way that individuals find personal meaning, but also as an attempt to influence the character of modernity—to make it more meaningful. What are the prospects for the "project of divinity"?

Max Weber, the first social theorist to talk about the problem of modern meaninglessness, identified *intellectual rationality* as the source of the problem. Jurgen Habermas and Anthony Giddens, the two main contemporary social theorists to talk about modern meaninglessness, have agreed with Weber that intellectual rationality prevents religion from being a compelling source of meaning in modern society. But the existence of reflexive spirituality suggests that the opposite can be true: intellectual rationality, instead of draining the meaning out of religion, can bring renewed meaning to religion. If reflexive spirituality is nothing else, it is an example of intellectually rational religion. Reflexive spiritualists use intellectual rationality to make religion more meaningful: to illuminate symbols that had seemed opaque, to mine the spiritual resources of previously unfamiliar religious traditions, and to make what had seemed like someone else's language "speak to us where we live." For reflexive spiritualists, intellectual rationality is not an obstacle to religious meaning—it is a resource for the creation of religious meaning. If intellectual rationality—reason—is the enemy of religious meaning in modern society, then reflexive spiritualists seem to have turned that enemy into a friend.

Habermas and Giddens agree with Weber that intellectual rationality rules out religion as a source of modern meaning, but for the most part, they blame modern meaninglessness on an overgrowth of *technological rationality*. Technological rationality is about finding the most efficient means to a given end; when we use this kind of rationality to create organizations, we get powerful bureaucratic systems like the ones that run our governments and corporations. Habermas and Giddens have each developed theories about how these bureaucratic systems make it difficult for people to find and create existential meaning. The emphases of their theories are different, but both scholars think that the key to regaining a sense of meaning lies in creating space for communication. We need settings where people can come together and talk about shared concerns, and these settings need to be free from the control of powerful bureaucracies and their utilitarian logic. They need to be spaces where people can come together for no other purpose than to talk with one another. In talking with one another freely, we create culture—we create meaning.[1]

Reflexive spiritualists are one part of this communication-based solution to the problem of modern meaninglessness. They gather together to talk together about shared concerns. And even more interesting, the shared concerns that they're talking about directly address questions of meaning and the patterns of technological rationality that make meaning difficult. Reflexive spirituality gives them a language, a way of talking explicitly about spiritual meaning in relation to modern life.

In Habermas's and Giddens's terms, two things would give reflexive spirituality a good chance of bringing renewed meaning to modern society. First, reflexive spiritualists need to have spaces to talk openly with one another so that they can continue to create spiritual meanings that make sense to them. And second, these conversations need to be buttressed by a host of other conversations all across society—conversations in which people come together to talk openly and respectfully about the things that matter to them. Technological rationality and the bureaucracies it creates are powerful, and reflexive spirituality alone can't counterbalance their power. But if we follow Habermas's and Giddens's logic, then reflexive spirituality is part of the solution to modern meaninglessness—one of the many kinds of meaningful conversations that members of modern societies need to have.

What Does Reflexive Spirituality Need to Thrive?

Habermas's and Giddens's emphasis on communication points to a practical resource that reflexive spirituality needs if it is to thrive: space for open communication. The conversations I observed took place in church basements, rented meeting rooms, retreat centers, and lecture halls, and over the radio and television airwaves. Many of these spaces were set up to privilege the voices of one person or a group of people as teachers or experts. This isn't necessarily a bad thing, especially because so many of them also incorporated discussion periods, question-and-answer segments, and breaks during which people could talk with one another more equally. And reflexivity is in part a cycle of learning from people who have delved deeply into particular topics, then considering their ideas individually and collectively. Still, reflexive spirituality requires not only lectures, speeches, sermons, and books, but also discussions and conversations.

As Habermas points out, and as Victor Turner's work on liminality also suggests, truly open, creative communication requires spaces that are not dominated by some powerful institutional bureaucracy.[2] Creative ideas emerge in the in-between spaces—the discussion groups; the workshops; and the small, hard-to-explain organizations like Common Ground. These ideas make their way into more powerful spaces like the pulpit, the mass media, and the workplace—and reflexive spiritualists are eager to see them there—but it's essential to maintain and cultivate those small, off-the-beaten-path spaces to keep the reflexivity alive.

My observations suggested a few other things that reflexive spirituality might need if it is to thrive. First, it needs to stay reflexive. Reflexive spiritualists need to keep questioning, keep rethinking, keep rearticulating their ideas, and keep considering new and potentially uncomfortable ideas. Technological rationality, with its emphasis on efficiency and quick answers, could potentially eat away at reflexive spirituality until it becomes its own dogma, complete with oversimplified sound bites: "It's a metaphor; you can't take it literally," "All religions are saying basically the same thing," "It doesn't matter what you believe; it's about who you are," "Ritual is just empty routine," "You can set your own rules," "It's about questions, not answers"—and "You can't put God in a box." When serious questions are met with stock phrases, the reflexive process is shut down and all the potential of open inquiry is lost. If reflexive spiritualists find themselves using these phrases to shut down inquiry rather than to promote it, they risk becoming just another distortion of technological rationality. And then it might be time to get back on track by asking, for example, "What if it *is* literally true? What important differences are there between religions? What do we actually believe, and how might that matter? What meaning does ritual have? How might rules be meaningful? When is it a good idea to come to a conclusion and hold it with conviction? So what if you can't put God in a box? What does that mean for living?"

A second thing that might help reflexive spirituality thrive is to articulate its commitments. Occasionally, when reflexive spiritualists speak, it sounds like "We don't believe this, and we don't believe that, and here's another thing that we don't believe." Articulating what reflexive spirituality *isn't* is the first step in marking out an identity, and sometimes it's the first step along the reflexive path. The second step is to go deeper: to talk about out what you *do* think, what you *do* stand for, and what you have to contribute. Reflexive spiritualists have a lot of creative and thoughtful ideas about spirituality, and the reflexive process ensures a continuing supply of these ideas. Ultimately, it's these ideas and this process that provide people with spiritual meaning.

It's a conundrum, really. When reflexive spiritualists emphasize what they don't believe, it's sometimes because they're talking to people who might be hearing these ideas for the first time. Sometimes, it's because opposing voices are so loud that they feel like they have to keep saying the same thing over and over again just to be heard. For example, so many Americans equate religion in general with particular expressions of Christian conservatism that reflexive Christians find themselves continually saying, "We're Christian, but not that kind of Christian" or "I'm religious, but not like that."

When reflexive spiritualists get a chance to say what they do think, it sometimes just sounds like a list. For example, when I go to church services and public talks by reflexive spiritualists, I sometimes find myself mentally checking off the boxes: there's the nonliteralism, there's the open stance toward multiple religions, there's the injunction to be open-minded. I know that there's more beneath the surface, but when you're continually having to do Reflexive Spirituality 101, it can be hard to move on to discuss your more complex spiritual ideas. But educated seekers are looking for that complexity; they're looking for spiritual depth. They often find that depth in the smaller spaces—the discussion groups, workshops, and classes. But if they only attend a Sunday service or a public lecture, they may not know that what reflexive spirituality is about is creating spiritual meaning.

A third way for reflexive spirituality to thrive is to communicate across religious boundaries. Over the past couple of decades, reflexive spiritualists within particular traditions have gradually become aware of one another and have begun to communicate with one another in an organized way. The Center for Progressive Christianity, for example, has brought together some reflexive Christians, and people who identify as progressive Christians are increasingly aware of themselves as an interdenominational movement within Christianity. Likewise, people who identify as spiritual but not religious have become aware of one another and have begun to seek each other out for community—for example, through the organization SBNR.[3] I suspect that reflexive spiritualists can also be found in the Jewish Renewal Movement and the Jewish Reconstructionist Federation. My sense is that reflexive spiritualists within these different traditions are often not aware that members of other traditions are engaged in parallel work. But each of them is one part of a larger, interreligious cultural and spiritual movement—they have allies in other traditions. It seems so consistent with reflexive spirituality's commitment to pluralism, not to mention its commitment to reflexive learning, that these organizations might want to talk with one another about their common spiritual interests.

Ultimately, what matters about reflexive spirituality is its relationship to meaning. Reflexive spirituality is one way that modern Americans are finding and making spiritual meaning—transcendent meaning, existential meaning, religious meaning—the "how does it all hang together" kind of meaning that helps people orient themselves to a chaotic world, an immense universe, and a life that we never could have predicted.

NOTES

PREFACE: MEANING, MIND, AND RELIGION IN TWO LIVES

1. "Mike Seaton" is a pseudonym.

CHAPTER 1

1. A few scholars whose work has addressed these questions: Ammerman, *Bible Believers*; Bellah, *Beyond Belief*; Giddens, *Consequences of Modernity*; Giddens, *Modernity and Self Identity*; Habermas, "Awareness of What is Missing"; Habermas, *Theory of Communicative Action*; Hunter, *American Evangelicalism*; Ricoeur, *Hermeneutics and the Human Sciences*; Ricoeur, *Philosophy of Paul Ricoeur*; Ricoeur, *Ricoeur Reader*; Ricoeur, *Symbolism of Evil*; Huston Smith, *Why Religion Matters*; Stark and Bainbridge, *The Future of Religion*; Taylor, *Secular Age*; Weber, *Economy and Society*; Weber, "Science as a Vocation."
2. Roof, *Spiritual Marketplace*. Jerome Baggett has also developed the concept of reflexive spirituality in *Sense of the Faithful*.
3. For more on reflexive spirituality as a culture, see Besecke, "Speaking of Meaning." For more on religion as a societal conversation, see Besecke, "Seeing Invisible Religion."
4. Giddens, *Consequences of Modernity*; Giddens, *Modernity and Self Identity*; Habermas, *Theory of Communicative Action*; Ricoeur, *Hermeneutics and the Human Sciences*; Ricoeur, *Philosophy of Paul Ricoeur*; Ricoeur, *Ricoeur Reader*; Ricoeur, *Symbolism of Evil*; Weber, *Economy and Society*; Weber, "Science as a Vocation." See discussion below and in Chapter 2.
5. I develop the idea of technological rationality and its relationship to meaning in Chapter 3.
6. Ricoeur, *Symbolism of Evil*, 350.
7. I develop the idea of intellectual rationality and its use by reflexive spiritualists in Chapter 5.
8. Bellah, *Beyond Belief*, 232–233.

9. Campbell, "Secret Religion"; Swatos, "Enchantment and Disenchantment"; Wuthnow, *After Heaven*, 5–8; Bender, *New Metaphysicals*, 83–84.

10. Baggett, *Sense of the Faithful*.

11. Roof, *Spiritual Marketplace*, 75.

12. Wuthnow, *After Heaven*, 6; Bender, *New Metaphysicals*, 84; Roof, *Spiritual Marketplace*, 100.

13. Thomas Luckmann, *Invisible Religion*.

14. I use Luckmann's examples throughout this paragraph, not only for clarity and accuracy, but also because I couldn't do better for entertainment value. All are from page 57 of *The Invisible Religion*.

15. Strauss and Corbin, *Basics of Qualitative Research*.

16. Throughout this book, I use the real names of organizations, organizational leaders, and major speakers. At First United Methodist Church, this includes David Lyons and Cecil Findley, introduced in this section, and Joan Deming, First Church's associate pastor at the time of my research. At Common Ground, this includes Ron Miller, Jim Kenney, and Wayne Teasdale, introduced in this section; and Ron Kidd and Philip Simmons, two additional Common Ground teachers. I use the real names of all the authors and event leaders in the secular settings I studied and the real first names of people who called in to ask questions during call-in radio interview programs. I use pseudonyms for everyone else that I quote, in part because I often did not know their real names. This includes participants in classes and events held at First Church, Common Ground, and the secular settings I studied.

17. The statistics I have on First United Methodist Church are from the church's annual report to the National United Methodist Church.

18. These quotations were featured on the Association for Spirit at Work Web site in 2002. ASAW later became the International Center for Spirit at Work, and in 2007, after fourteen years, decided to become dormant (http://www.spiritatwork.org).

19. I believe that the Crossroads Center is also now defunct.

20. See Besecke, "Seeing Invisible Religion" for more about my use of Luckmann's theory. On liminality, see Turner, *Blazing the Trail*; *Dramas, Fields, and Metaphors*; *Forest of Symbols*; *From Ritual to Theatre*; *Ritual Process*.

21. For communication-centered concepts of culture, see Eliasoph, *Avoiding Politics*; Eliasoph and Lichterman, "Culture in Interaction"; Wuthnow, *Vocabularies*; and Wuthnow, *Rediscovering the Sacred*. For reflexive spirituality as a language, see Besecke, "Speaking of Meaning."

22. Strauss and Corbin, *Basics of Qualitative Research*.

23. Ibid.

24. Burawoy, *Ethnography Unbound*; Burawoy, "The Extended Case Method"; Eliasoph and Lichterman, "We Begin with our Favorite Theory."

25. For example, see Berger, *Sacred Canopy*; Bruce, *God is Dead*; Bruce, *Religion in the Modern World*; Bruce, *Secularization*; Chaves, "Secularization as Declining Religious Authority"; Finke and Stark, "Evaluating the Evidence"; Finke and Stark, *The*

Churching of America; Giddens, *Consequences of Modernity*; Giddens, *Modernity and Self-Identity*; Habermas, *Theory of Communicative Action*; Heelas, *New Age Movement*; Hunter, *American Evangelicalism*; Wilson, *Religion in Secular Society*.

Max Weber did consider how religion might affect modernity, most notably in *The Protestant Ethic and the Spirit of Capitalism*. Weber theorized a causal effect of Calvinism on capitalism and other forms of societal rationalization, and imagined a consequential demise of spirituality. Religion, once it created modernity, would wither away, killed by its own offspring. Very lately, scholars have begun to think about how religious groups—especially conservative religious groups—might affect the political character of modernity (Casanova, *Public Religions*; Habermas, "Awareness of What is Missing"). Since Weber, though, scholars haven't really thought much about how religion might affect modernity's spiritual character.

26. Weber, *Economy and Society*, "Science as a Vocation"; Habermas, *Theory of Communicative Action*; Giddens, *Consequences of Modernity, Modernity and Self-Identity*.

27. Ricoeur, *Hermeneutics and the Human Sciences*; Ricoeur, *Philosophy of Paul Ricoeur*; Ricoeur, *Ricoeur Reader*; Ricoeur, *Symbolism of Evil*.

CHAPTER 2

1. Hoff, *The Tao of Pooh*, 134.
2. Weber, "Science as a Vocation," 155. Some sociologists would use Karl Marx's word "alienation" instead of "disenchantment" to highlight the dehumanizing effects of capitalism. Weber's theory is broader than this: he considers capitalism to be just one of several important forms of rationalization and gives serious attention to transcendent meaning and religious change. For these reasons, and because this book is about the relationship between reason and transcendent meaning, I use Weber's terminology.
3. Berger, *Sacred Canopy*; Durkheim, *Division of Labor*; Durkheim, *Elementary Forms*; Habermas, *Theory of Communicative Action*; Luckmann, *Invisible Religion*; Weber, *Economy and Society*.
4. Berger, *Sacred Canopy*.
5. Weber, "Science as a Vocation"; see also Giddens, *Modernity and Self-Identity*, and Habermas, *Theory of Communicative Action*.
6. Giddens, *Modernity and Self-Identity*, 3.
7. Dorrien, *The Making of American Liberal Theology*; Ricoeur, *Philosophy of Paul Ricoeur*; Ricoeur, *Ricoeur Reader*; Ricoeur, *Symbolism of Evil*; Weber, *Economy and Society*.
8. Fuller, *Spiritual But Not Religious*; Roof, *Spiritual Marketplace*; Wuthnow, *After Heaven*; see also Albanese, *Republic of Mind and Spirit*; Bellah, Madsen, Sullivan, Swidler, and Tipton, *Habits of the Heart*; Bender, *New Metaphysicals*; Schmidt, *Restless Souls*.

9. Berger, *Sacred Canopy*; Bruce, *God Is Dead*; Bruce, *Religion in the Modern World*; Bruce, *Secularization*; Chaves, "Secularization"; Dobbelaere, "Integrated Perspective"; Hunter, *American Evangelicalism*; Luckmann, *Invisible Religion*; Tschannen, "Secularization Paradigm," Wilson, *Contemporary Transformations*; Wilson, *Religion in Secular Society*; Wilson, *Religion in Sociological Perspective*; Wilson, "Secularization"; Yamane, "Secularization on Trial." Nancy Ammerman's *Bible Believers* describes fundamentalist Christians who self-consciously position themselves against modernity.

10. Sociologists, too, sometimes equate religious conservatism with religious strength; see Smith, *American Evangelicalism*; Stark and Bainbridge, *Future of Religion*.

11. Habermas, *Philosophical Discourse*.

12. Taylor, *Secular Age*, and Habermas, "Awareness of What Is Missing" hint at the possibility that religious perspectives might point up some of the limitations of narrowly rationalistic perspectives. But the best philosophical statements on this topic come from Paul Ricoeur, whose work directly addressed the complex relationship between rationality and religious meaning. For Ricoeur, some modes of rationality constrain meaningfulness by treating literalism as the height of truthfulness, while other modes of rationality can promote meaningfulness by helping us become aware of possibilities of interpretation. See Ricoeur, *Hermeneutics and the Human Sciences*; Ricoeur, "Hermeneutics of Symbols"; Ricoeur, *Philosophy of Paul Ricoeur*; Ricoeur, *Ricoeur Reader*; Ricoeur, *Symbolism of Evil*. Approaching the subject from a different angle, some of the work that emerged from the 1960s counterculture pointed out limitations of rationality associated with the rise of technology; see, for example, Roszak, *Making of a Counter Culture*.

13. Dorrien, *Making of American Liberal Theology, 1805–1900; 1900–1950*; and *1950–2005*. See also Dorrien, *Word as True Myth* and Hodgson, *Liberal Theology*.

14. Dorrien, *Making of American Liberal Theology, 1900–1950*, 3.

15. For more on scientism and religion, see Smith, *Why Religion Matters*.

16. For example, Finke and Stark, *Churching of America*; Stark and Bainbridge, *Future of Religion*; Troeltsch, *Social Teachings of the Christian Churches*.

17. Dorrien, *Making of American Liberal Theology 1950–2005*, 513.

18. This idea of the recovery of myth as a language of truth also appears in popular books by Karen Armstrong (*Battle for God, History of God*), Joseph Campbell (*The Power of Myth*), and Huston Smith (*Why Religion Matters*).

19. Jewish Reconstructionist Federation, "Is reconstructionist Judaism for you?" http://jrf.org.

20. Aleph: Alliance for Jewish Renewal, "Statement of Principles," http://www.aleph.org/about.htm.

21. Courtney Bender, in *The New Metaphysicals*, points out that the spirituality movement is sustained by a variety of institutions, practices, and discourses that we ordinarily think of as secular. Leigh Eric Schmidt, in *Restless Souls*, provides a history of unchurched spirituality in the United States; and Robert Fuller, in *Spiritual But*

Not Religious, analyzes some of the American spirituality movement's themes. See also Albanese, *Republic of Mind and Spirit*; Heelas, *New Age Movement*; Kripal, *Esalen*; and Porterfield, *Transformation of American Religion*.

22. For more information on the Baby Boomer generation and the American spirituality movement, see Roof, *Generation of Seekers*; Roof, *Spiritual Marketplace*; Tipton, *Getting Saved from the Sixties*; Wuthnow, *After Heaven*; Wuthnow, *Restructuring of American Religion*. See also Bellah et al., *Habits of the Heart*; Kripal, *Esalen*; and Roszak, *Making of a Counter Culture*.

23. I've drawn the historical information in this section from Albanese, *Republic of Mind and Spirit*; Fuller, *Religious Revolutionaries*; Fuller, *Spiritual But Not Religious*; and Schmidt, *Restless Souls*.

24. Fuller, *Religious Revolutionaries*, 94.

25. See Swidler, *Talk of Love*, for more on the idea of culture as a repertoire of symbolic ideas.

CHAPTER 3

1. Lyrics excerpted from "Crescent Moon," by Chris Cunningham and Johnny Hermanson, Chris and Johnny Live at the Grand, 1993 Story Hills Music, Inc. http://storyhill.com.

2. Behold my attempt to summarize the intricate theories of Habermas and Giddens together in one sentence. Habermas discusses technological rationality in the course of his discussion of the system and the lifeworld in *Theory of Communicative Action*. "Systems" are built on formal rationality, the creation of institutional structures that use rules, regulations, procedures, and hierarchies to efficiently pursue desired ends. The technological rationality that I'm talking about is one component of formal rationality. For Habermas, it is the overgrowth of these systems and the logic they promote that drains meaning out of modern society. Giddens discusses technological rationality in *Modernity and Self-Identity* as part of the specialization fostered by the growth of formal organizations. He sees formal rationality as "squeezing to the sidelines" the kinds of experiences that might allow people to raise questions of meaning. Reflexive spiritualists share with these two theorists the idea that we're experiencing a kind of cancerous overgrowth, a takeover, an overreliance on technological rationality, and that this overgrowth is robbing us of the social and cultural resources that we need to ensure meaningfulness.

3. See Ricoeur, *Hermeneutics and the Human Sciences*; Ricoeur, *Philosophy of Paul Ricoeur*; Ricoeur, *Ricoeur Reader*; Ricoeur, *Symbolism of Evil*.

4. Lyrics from "I am a Lover," by Chris Cunningham and Johnny Hermanson, Shapeshifting, 1991 Story Hills Music, Inc. http://storyhill.com.

5. I think this is why people so often use the word "literally" incorrectly, as in "I literally died of embarrassment." If the literal truth is "more true" than the figurative

truth, then it makes sense to use "literally" for emphasis; it just means "take me seriously; I really mean it; I'm not kidding—this is true." If I said, "I figuratively died of embarrassment," it just wouldn't pack the same punch, because we live in a society that sees figurative truths as less serious, less real, than literal truths.

6. Bellah, *Beyond Belief.*
7. Lyrics excerpted from "Universe Communion," by Stuart Davis, Self-Untitled, 1994, Panacea Records. http://www.stuartdavis.com.
8. Smith, *Why Religion Matters*, 59–60.
9. Ricoeur, *Ricoeur Reader*, 452.
10. Ricoeur, *Philosophy of Paul Ricoeur*, 224.
11. Gunther, "God and Business."

CHAPTER 4

1. Maslow, *Psychology of Science*, 15.
2. The New Age specter is especially powerful in academia, that bastion of technological reason. In academia, the phrase "New Agey" has very little to do with the actual New Age movement; it seems instead to describe spiritualities that depart from familiar religious language and that take place outside traditional religious institutions. The New Age specter haunted this book from its beginnings. When I first began to articulate the book's topic, colleagues repeatedly brought up the New Age movement and advised me to distinguish my work from it; otherwise, they told me, I risked not being taken seriously as a scholar. Later, as I was writing initial drafts, an early reader suggested that I try to make the people I observed sound "less New Agey" since "most academics run from New Age type thinking like the plague." Apparently, even *studying* spiritual culture is suspicious. In reality, reflexive spirituality has some things in common with the New Age movement: both promote pluralism and mysticism, and both talk about an abstract and immanent divinity (see Chapter 6). And it differs from the New Age in many ways; for example, reflexive spirituality has a distinct intellectual tone while the New Age has a more individualistic tone, and reflexive spiritualists talk much more about religious tradition and much less about metaphysical phenomena. More to the point, the New Age is a religion, whereas reflexive spirituality is a way of relating to religious tradition. So a reflexive New Age movement is a theoretical possibility—for example, reflexive New Agers might discuss the metaphorical significance of common New Age topics such as aliens, divination, and auras. Some psychologists do just that kind of metaphorical interpretation in the course of their counseling work: see Keith Thompson, "UFO Encounter Experience."
3. Bender, *New Metaphysicals*, 66.
4. Ibid., 68–70.
5. Ken Wilber is often associated with the word "transrationality," although he is not at all the only person to discuss this idea. The Common Ground teachers were

familiar with Wilber's work and may have been thinking of it when they discussed transrationality, although Ron didn't mention him in this context.

6. A few of the sociologists who have discussed this idea of language making things culturally real are Bellah et al., *Habits of the Heart*; Berger and Luckmann, *Social Construction of Reality*; Besecke, *Seeing Invisible Religion*; and Wuthnow, *Acts of Compassion*.

CHAPTER 5

1. This understanding of intellectual reason is grounded on Habermas, *Theory of Communicative Action*; Weber, *Economy and Society*; and Weber, "Science as a Vocation." But for intellectual reason's capacity to renew religious tradition, see Ricoeur, *Hermeneutics and the Human Sciences*, Ricoeur, "Hermeneutics of Symbols"; Ricoeur, *Philosophy of Paul Ricoeur*; Ricoeur, *Ricoeur Reader*; Ricoeur, *Symbolism of Evil*.

2. Giddens, *Modernity and Self-Identity*, 3.

3. Baggett, *Sense of the Faithful*, describes reflexive Catholics engaging in this same kind of thoughtful consideration of official theology; he describes reflexivity as a "negotiation" in which reflexive Catholics take official interpretations seriously but do not treat them as totally authoritative; they feel free to reject official interpretations that do not accord with their own understanding of Catholic theology. Dillon, *Catholic Identity*, describes pro-change Catholics rejecting aspects of Catholic moral doctrine as a result of a reflexive process in which they identify some aspects of doctrine as in conflict with other, more important aspects of doctrine. I discuss both of these books in Chapter 7.

4. The "religious studies ethos" also promotes religious pluralism, an important dimension of reflexive spirituality that I discuss later in this chapter.

5. Baggett, *Sense of the Faithful*; Dillon, *Catholic Identity*; Dillon, "Authority of the Holy"; Dorrien, *The Making of American Liberal Theology*.

6. Because of a disciplinary sensitivity to secularization and individualism, sociologists have often remarked on "the declining scope of religious authority" (Bruce, *God is Dead*; Bruce, *Religion in the Modern World*; Bruce, *Secularization*; Chaves, "Secularization"; Dobbelaere, "Towards an Integrated Perspective"; Yamane, "Secularization on Trial") and on individuals' increasing "independence from religious authority" (Bellah et al., *Habits of the Heart*; Berger, *Sacred Canopy*; Tamney, *Resilience of Christianity*). Usually, the fact that churches don't have complete interpretive authority over religious meaning is taken as evidence of religious decline. But as we see here, when members of the religious public take some of their interpretive authority back from specialist institutions, they sometimes find themselves more engaged with religious meanings, more spiritually creative, and more committed to the renewal of religious tradition.

7. Stark and Bainbridge, *Future of Religion* and Smith, *American Evangelicalism* imply that literal interpretations of religious scriptures are signs of religious strength; many

conservative religious leaders agree. Reflexive spiritualists, by contrast, find religious strength in metaphor because they find metaphor to be more evocative of meaning. This is not to imply that reflexive spiritualists don't believe in or find strength in any literal interpretations; they just reject the idea that literalism in general is the most powerful approach to religion.

8. Ricoeur, *Symbolism of Evil*, 170. Ricoeur is the master of metaphor, by which I mean not that he's really good at creating metaphors, but that his work does an excellent job of explaining how powerful metaphor is for evoking meaning. Joseph Campbell's work (for example, *Power of Myth*) brought this understanding of metaphor to the general public.

9. For example, Habermas, *Theory of Communicative Action*, vol. 1, 43–53; Ricoeur, *Symbolism of Evil*, 10–14, 161–166.

10. Again, the best philosophical statement of these ideas comes from Paul Ricoeur, who said that religious texts are meaningful to the extent that we are able to imaginatively enter the worlds they evoke. Meaning, for Ricoeur, lies not "behind the text"—as in literalistic and reductionistic attempts to get at "the real meaning"— but "in front of the text," in the worlds the text suggests. Meaning enters as we leave behind the prejudices of our own culture to consider the possible ways of being that the text implies. See Ricoeur, *Hermeneutics and the Human Sciences*; Ricoeur, "Hermeneutics of Symbols"; Ricoeur, *Philosophy of Paul Ricoeur*; Ricoeur, *Ricoeur Reader*; and Ricoeur, *Symbolism of Evil*.

11. Ricoeur, *Symbolism of Evil*, 161.

12. Lyrics to "The Birthday Party" by Peter Mayer, Bountiful, 1997, ASCAP. http://www.blueboat.net.

13. This distinction between truth and the language we use to try to express it has been explored in different ways by philosophers ranging from Wittgenstein to Foucault. In sociology, this distinction has been most important in the sociology of knowledge (for example, Berger and Luckmann, *Social Construction of Reality*) and cultural sociology (for example, Bellah et al., *Habits of the Heart* and Wuthnow, *Acts of Compassion*).

14. Some secularization theories have imagined religious commitment as an unquestioning adherence to a single, overarching tradition; Berger, *Sacred Canopy* is the definitive statement of this perspective. The "religious economies" perspective, by contrast, suggests that the existence of multiple religious options within a society can increase religious commitment through the power of choice; see for example Finke and Stark, "Evaluating the Evidence"; Finke and Stark, *The Churching of America*; Smith, *American Evangelicalism*. In both these approaches, the religiously committed person is imagined to associate with one religion and either to be unaware of or to reject other religions. Reflexive spiritualists are different. Some of them adhere to a particular religion and draw on other religions to enrich their experience of their religion, some actively engage in more than one religion, and others don't adhere to any particular religious tradition. In my observations,

those who did identify with one particular religious tradition described their investigations of other religious perspectives as facilitating their commitment to their own tradition by enlivening it. "The Buddhist definition of grace is one of the best definitions I've seen and really helps my own understanding of Christian grace," said one member of First Church's Religions of the World class. Despite our very different approaches, my observations of reflexive spirituality and the religious-economies scholars' observations of historical changes both support the general idea that pluralism can enliven religious life and strengthen religious engagement.

15. Stephen Prothero (*God Is Not One*) and others have expressed concern that emphasizing religious similarities can lead to a too-facile denial of religious difference, as in "religions are all the same anyway" and "they're all describing the same God in the end." For Prothero, it's important to understand religions objectively, as social forces. What do different religions lead people and communities to do? How do their emphases differ? How do they lead people to understand the world? In a world where religious violence is frontstage, Prothero's desire to promote the understanding of religious difference is absolutely called for. But reflexive spiritualists (as well as many of the "religious universalists" he discusses) are thinking more about facilitating spiritual meaning than about understanding diverse populations; they approach religious traditions as the heritage of us all. It's a matter of focus and emphasis. Reflexive spirituality takes a more "internal" approach to religious traditions: the goal is to create spiritual meaning. Prothero takes a more "external" approach: the goal is to understand diverse others. To put it another way, Prothero wants his readers to learn *about* the world's religions; reflexive spiritualists want to learn *from* the world's religions. If reflexive spiritualists were to read *God Is Not One*, as I'm sure many of them have, they would probably come away with a stronger understanding of the importance of religious difference. But what they would really value would be the sense of what they themselves, and their own spiritual communities, could learn from each of these different traditions. And they'd still believe that the divine is greater than any one religion's conceptualization of it.

16. I discuss this variation and other differences between my field sites in Chapter 7.

17. Campbell, "Secret Religion"; Roof, *Generation of Seekers*; Roof, "Modernity, the Religious, and the Spiritual"; Roof, *Spiritual Marketplace*; Roof, "Toward the Year 2000"; Swatos, "Enchantment and Disenchantment"; Troeltsch, *Social Teachings*.

18. Wuthnow, *After Heaven*.

19. Sociologists who have expressed these kinds of concerns include Bellah et al., *Habits of the Heart* and Wuthnow, *Acts of Compassion*.

20. In *The New Metaphysicals*, Courtney Bender describes this way of thinking about mysticism—as a kind of asociological or presocial event around which religious traditions form—as a story scholars tell that has gotten in the way of a sociology of spiritual experience. Sociologists in general would point out that experience

always takes place in a social context and that social contexts facilitate different kinds of experiences. Reflexive spiritualists also recognize the importance of social context—thus their criticisms of modern social patterns that inhibit and invalidate spiritual experiences. The difference is in what each group is really interested in: sociologists want to understand the social contexts that produce mystical experiences and discourses about them, while reflexive spiritualists want the transcendent meaning offered by mystical experiences themselves.

CHAPTER 6

1. Ricoeur, *Symbolism of Evil*, 349.
2. Stuart Davis, "Universe Communion," *Self-Untitled*, Panacea Records, 1994, http://www.stuartdavis.com. The emotional tone I'm describing isn't unique to reflexive spirituality; readers will recognize this energy as common to many people who believe they possess valuable insight that others don't see as valuable ("You just don't get it"). In *Bible Believers*, for example, Nancy Ammerman noted that the fundamentalist Christians she studied had a similar sense of the larger society being "willfully deaf." But reflexive spirituality has such a strong intellectual tone that it's important to recognize the ways that it's not only about the mind.
3. One of Smith's other books is called *Cleansing the Doors of Perception*.
4. Stark and Bainbridge, *Future of Religion*, 107, 429–430.
5. *Ibid.*, 81.
6. I'm no theologian, and to really delve into the nuances of how different liberal Christians and theologians have interpreted the crucifixion and the atonement is way beyond the scope of this book. A few references for the interested: Brock and Parker, *Proverbs of Ashes*; Dorrien, *Making of American Liberal Theology*; Jones, *Better Atonement*; Wink, *Powers That Be*. For the reflexive spiritualists that I studied, the main point wasn't the role that Jesus's crucifixion may have played in atonement. Rather, the main point was that people can experience themselves as "at one" with the divine.
7. Huston Smith also makes this point in *Why Religion Matters*. He argues, "The issue between science and religion is not between facts and values. . . . The fundamental issue is about facts, period. . . . It is about the standing of values in the objective world, the world that is there whether human beings exist or not. Are values as deeply ingrained in that world as are its natural laws, or are they added to it as epiphenomenal gloss when life enters the picture?" (71). Smith's position is that values—meaning—are inherent (immanent) in the world.
8. Simmons, *Learning to Fall*, 62–63.
9. Excerpted from T.S. Eliot, "The Waste Land."
10. I probably got this phrase from the title of Marcus Borg's book *The God We Never Knew*.
11. Giddens, *Modernity and Self-Identity*, 20.

CHAPTER 7

1. Courtney Bender observed a similar pattern in the spirituality movement in Cambridge, Massachusetts: as she put it, "Daily life was . . . always possibly revelatory" (Bender, *New Metaphysicals*, 83).

2. Very briefly, *inclusivists* believe that one religion is fully true, while other religions are partly true, and *exclusivists* believe that one religion is true and all others are false. *Relativists* believe that there is no absolute truth, that truth can only be subjective, and that what any individual or group considers to be true depends on their unique circumstances or frame of reference. *Pluralism* has various meanings, but for reflexive spiritualists, it means a belief that all religions reveal truth and that none is a priori superior to the others.

3. Michele Dillon, "Authority of the Holy Revisited," 297.

4. Jerome Baggett, *Sense of the Faithful*, 101.

5. *Ibid.*, 80.

6. *Ibid.*, 76–78.

7. *Ibid.*, 100.

8. *Ibid.*, 112–113.

9. *Ibid.*, 106.

10. *Ibid.*, 84.

11. Eugene Kennedy, *Tomorrow's Catholics*, 21, quoted in Baggett, *Sense of the Faithful*, 104.

12. Shapiro, *Minyan*.

13. Rabbi Shapiro went on to cofound the One River Wisdom School, http://oneriverwisdomschool.com.

14. ALEPH: Alliance for Jewish Renewal, "ALEPH Statement of Principles," http://www.aleph.org/principles.htm (accessed June 4, 2012).

15. Jewish Reconstructionist Federation, "Is Reconstructionist Judaism For You?" October 16, 2007, http://jrf.org/showres&rid = 141 (accessed June 4, 2012).

16. The idea of reflexive spirituality as a set of meaning-making tools is probably informed by Ann Swidler's classic article about culture as a tool kit ("Culture in Action"); she further developed this idea in *Talk of Love*, using the concept of cultural repertoires. See also Besecke, "Speaking of Meaning," about reflexive spirituality as a cultural resource. See Eliasoph and Lichterman, "Culture in Interaction," for more about how group membership mediates people's use of collective representations. Eliasoph and Lichterman use individualism as their primary example of a collective representation; reflexive spirituality may be a collective representation that different groups practice differently depending on their group style.

CHAPTER 8

1. Very briefly, Habermas calls these bureaucracies and their peculiar logic *the system* and says that this system has infiltrated spaces where it doesn't belong—spaces

where people can communicate openly, connect with one another as human beings, and come to shared understandings. (He calls these spaces for shared communication *the lifeworld*.) Giddens, meanwhile, thinks that complex, narrowly focused bureaucracies separate people from the kinds of life situations that give rise to conversation about existential meanings. More than ever before, our medical systems, criminal justice systems, urban design systems, and other systems keep life ordinary and routine by keeping it relatively separate from the existential challenges presented by things like mental and physical illness, criminality, death, and nature. Both theorists look to the political sphere for solutions—Habermas wants to revitalize spaces for people to communicate as citizens, and Giddens advocates a "life politics" that would refocus attention on existential questions. These scholars look to the political realm in part because they have discounted the religious realm as hopelessly traditionalistic and resistant to reflexivity. They're wrong about that, but their broader ideas about the importance of meaningful communication remain compelling.

2. See Chapter 1 for my sense of how Victor Turner's work speaks to the question of where people create countercultural meanings.

3. http://www.sbnr.org.

BIBLIOGRAPHY

Albanese, Catherine L. *A Republic of Mind and Spirit: A Cultural History of American Metaphysical Religion*. New Haven, CT: Yale University Press, 2007.

Ammerman, Nancy. *Bible Believers: Fundamentalists in the Modern World*. New Brunswick, NJ: Rutgers University Press, 1987.

Armstrong, Karen. *The Battle for God*. New York: Ballantine, 2000.

———. *A History of God: The 4000-Year Quest of Judaism, Christianity, and Islam*. New York: Ballantine, 1993.

Baggett, Jerome P. *Sense of the Faithful: How American Catholics Live Their Faith*. New York: Oxford University Press, 2009.

Bellah, Robert N. *Beyond Belief: Essays on Religion in a Post-Traditional World*. New York: Harper & Row, 1970.

Bellah, Robert N., Richard Madsen, William M. Sullivan, Ann Swidler, and Steven M. Tipton. *Habits of the Heart: Individualism and Commitment in American Life*. Berkeley: University of California Press, 1985.

Bender, Courtney. *The New Metaphysicals: Spirituality and the American Religious Imagination*. Chicago: University of Chicago Press, 2010.

Berger, Peter L. *The Sacred Canopy: Elements of a Sociological Theory of Religion*. New York: Anchor Books, 1967.

Berger, Peter L., and Thomas Luckmann. *The Social Construction of Reality: A Treatise in the Sociology of Knowledge*. New York: Anchor Books, 1966.

Besecke, Kelly. "Seeing Invisible Religion: Religion as a Societal Conversation about Transcendent Meaning." *Sociological Theory* 23, no. 2 (2005): 179–196.

———. "Speaking of Meaning in Modernity: Reflexive Spirituality as a Cultural Resource." *Sociology of Religion* 62, no. 3 (2001): 365–381.

Borg, Marcus. *The God We Never Knew: Beyond Dogmatic Religion to a More Authentic Contemporary Faith*. New York: HarperOne, 1998.

Brock, Rita Nakashima, and Rebecca Ann Parker. *Proverbs of Ashes: Violence, Redemptive Suffering, and the Search for What Saves Us*. Boston: Beacon, 2001.

Bruce, Steve. *God Is Dead: Secularization in the West*. Malden, MA: Blackwell, 2002.

Bruce, Steve. *Religion in the Modern World: From Cathedrals to Cults.* New York: Oxford University Press, 1996.

———. *Secularization: In Defense of an Unfashionable Theory.* New York: Oxford University Press, 2011.

Burawoy, Michael. *Ethnography Unbound.* Berkeley: University of California Press, 1991.

———. "The Extended Case Method." *Sociological Theory* 16, no. 1 (1998): 4–33.

Campbell, Colin. "The Secret Religion of the Educated Classes." *Sociological Analysis* 39 (1978): 146–156.

Campbell, Joseph, with Bill Moyers. *The Power of Myth,* edited by Betty Sue Flowers. New York: Doubleday, 1988.

Casanova, Jose. *Public Religions in the Modern World.* Chicago: University of Chicago Press, 1994.

Chaves, Mark. "Secularization as Declining Religious Authority." *Social Forces* 72 (1994): 749–774.

Dillon, Michele. "The Authority of the Holy Revisited: Habermas, Religion, and Emancipatory Possibilities." *Sociological Theory* 17, no. 3 (1999): 290–306.

———. *Catholic Identity: Balancing Reason, Faith, and Power.* New York: Cambridge University Press, 1999.

Dobbelaere, Karel. "Towards an Integrated Perspective of the Processes Related to the Descriptive Concept of Secularization." *Sociology of Religion* 60, no. 3 (1999): 229–248.

Dorrien, Gary. *The Making of American Liberal Theology: Crisis, Irony, and Postmodernity, 1950–2005.* Louisville, KY: Westminster John Knox, 2006.

———. *The Making of American Liberal Theology: Idealism, Realism, & Modernity, 1900–1950.* Louisville, KY: Westminster John Knox, 2003.

———. *The Making of American Liberal Theology: Imagining Progressive Religion, 1805–1900.* Louisville, KY: Westminster John Knox, 2001.

———. *The Word as True Myth: Interpreting Liberal Theology.* Louisville, KY: Westminster John Knox, 1997.

Durkheim, Emile. *The Division of Labor in Society.* New York: Palgrave, 1984 [1893].

———. *The Elementary Forms of the Religious Life.* New York: Free Press, 1965 [1912].

Eliasoph, Nina. *Avoiding Politics: How Americans Produce Apathy in Everyday Life.* New York: Cambridge University Press, 1998.

Eliasoph, Nina, and Paul Lichterman. "Culture in Interaction." *American Journal of Sociology* 108, no. 4 (January 2003): 735–794.

———. "'We Begin with our Favorite Theory . . .' Reconstructing the Extended Case Method." *Sociological Theory* 17, no. 2 (1999): 228–234.

Finke, Roger, and Rodney Stark. *The Churching of America, 1776–1990: Winners and Losers in Our Religious Economy.* New Brunswick, NJ: Rutgers University Press, 1992.

———. "Evaluating the Evidence: Religious Economies and Sacred Canopies." *American Sociological Review* 54, no. 6 (1989): 1054–1057.

Fuller, Robert C. *Religious Revolutionaries: The Rebels Who Reshaped American Religion*. New York: Palgrave Macmillan, 2004.

———. *Spiritual But Not Religious: Understanding Unchurched America*. New York: Oxford University Press, 2001.

Giddens, Anthony. *The Consequences of Modernity*. Stanford, CA: Stanford University Press, 1990.

———. "Living in a Post-Traditional Society." In *Reflexive Modernization: Politics, Tradiiton and Aesthetics in the Modern Social Order*, edited by Ulrich Beck, Anthony Giddens, and Scott Lash. Stanford, CA: Stanford University Press, 1994, pp. 56–109.

———. *Modernity and Self-Identity: Self and Society in the Late Modern Age*. Cambridge: Polity Press, 1991.

Greeley, Andrew M. *Religion as Poetry*. New Brunswick, NJ: Transaction Publishers, 1996.

Gunther, Marc. "God and Business." *Fortune*. July 9, 2001: 59–80.

Habermas, Jurgen. "An Awareness of What Is Missing." In *An Awareness of What is Missing: Faith and Reason in a Post-Secular Age*, trans. Ciaran Cronin. Malden, MA: Polity Press, 2010, pp. 15–23.

———. "Modernity—An Incomplete Project." In *The Anti-Aesthetic: Essays on Postmodern Culture*, edited by Hal Foster. New York: New Press, 2002, pp. 3–15.

———. *The Philosophical Discourse of Modernity: Twelve Lectures*, trans. Frederick G. Lawrence. Cambridge, MA: MIT Press, 1990.

———. *The Theory of Communicative Action, vol. 1: Reason and the Rationalization of Society*. Boston: Beacon Press, 1984 [1981].

———. *The Theory of Communicative Action, vol. 2: Lifeworld and System: A Critique of Functionalist Reason*. Boston: Beacon Press, 1987 [1981].

Heelas, Paul. *The New Age Movement: The Celebration of the Self and the Sacralization of Modernity*. Cambridge, MA: Blackwell, 1996.

Hodgson, Peter C. *Liberal Theology: A Radical Vision*. Minneapolis: Augsburg Fortress, 2007.

Hoff, Benjamin. *The Tao of Pooh*. New York: Dutton, 1982.

Hunter, James Davison. *American Evangelicalism: Conservative Religion and the Quandary of Modernity*. New Brunswick, NJ: Rutgers University Press, 1983.

James, William. *The Varieties of Religious Experience*. New York: Random House, 1902.

Jones, Tony. *A Better Atonement: Beyond the Depraved Doctrine of Original Sin*. Minneapolis: JoPa Group, 2012.

Kennedy, Eugene. *Tomorrow's Catholics, Yesterday's Church: The Two Cultures of American Catholicism*. New York: Harper and Row, 1988.

Kripal, Jeffrey J. *Esalen: America and the Religion of No Religion*. Chicago: University of Chicago Press, 2007.

Luckmann, Thomas. *The Invisible Religion: The Problem of Religion in Modern Society*. New York: Macmillan, 1967.

Maslow, Abraham. *The Psychology of Science: A Reconnaissance*. New York: HarperCollins, 1966.

Porterfield, Amanda. *The Transformation of American Religion: The Story of a Late-Twentieth-Century Awakening*. New York: Oxford, 2001.

Prothero, Stephen. *God Is Not One: The Eight Rival Religions That Run the World*. New York: HarperOne, 2010.

Ricoeur, Paul. *Hermeneutics and the Human Sciences: Essays on Language, Action, and Interpretation*, edited by John B. Thompson. New York: Cambridge University Press, 1981.

———. "The Hermeneutics of Symbols and Philosophical Reflection: I." In *The Conflict of Interpretations: Essays in Hermeneutics*, edited by Done Ihde. Evanston: Northwestern University Press, 1974, pp. 284–311.

———. *The Philosophy of Paul Ricoeur: An Anthology of His Work*, edited by Charles E. Reagan and David Steward. Boston: Beacon Press, 1978.

———. *A Ricoeur Reader: Reflection and Imagination*, edited by Mario J. Valdes. Toronto: University of Toronto Press, 1991.

———. *The Symbolism of Evil*. New York: Harper & Row, 1967.

Roof, Wade Clark. *A Generation of Seekers: The Spiritual Journeys of the Baby Boom Generation*. New York: Harper SanFransisco, 1994.

———. "Modernity, the Religious, and the Spiritual." *Annals of the American Academy of Political and Social Science* 558 (1998): 211–224.

———. *Spiritual Marketplace: Baby Boomers and the Remaking of American Religion*. Princeton: Princeton University Press, 1999.

———. "Toward the Year 2000: Reconstructions of Religious Space." Annals of the American Academy of Political and Social Science 527 (1993): 155–170.

Roszak, Theodore. *The Making of a Counter Culture: Reflections on a Technocratic Society and Its Youthful Opposition*. New York: Anchor, 1969.

Schmidt, Leigh Eric. *Restless Souls: The Making of American Spirituality*. New York: Harper SanFrancisco, 2005.

Shapiro, Rami. *Minyan: Ten Principles for Living a Life of Integrity*. New York: Three Rivers Press, 1997.

Shapiro, Rami. *Minyan: Ten Principles for Living a Life of Integrity*. New York: Random House Digital, 2010.

Simmons, Philip. *Learning to Fall: The Blessings of an Imperfect Life*. New York: Bantam, 2000.

Smith, Christian. *American Evangelicalism: Embattled and Thriving*. Chicago: University of Chicago Press, 1998.

Smith, Huston. *Why Religion Matters: The Fate of the Human Spirit in an Age of Disbelief*. New York: Harper SanFrancisco, 2001.

Stark, Rodney, and W.S. Bainbridge. *The Future of Religion*. Berkeley: University of California Press, 1985.

Strauss, Anselm, and Juliet Corbin. *Basics of Qualitative Research: Grounded Theory Procedures and Techniques*. Newbury Park, CA: SAGE, 1990.

Swatos, William H. Jr. "Enchantment and Disenchantment in Modernity: The Significance of 'Religion' as a Sociocultural Category." *Sociological Analysis* 44 (1983): 321–338.

Swidler, Ann. "Culture in Action: Symbols and Strategies." *American Sociological Review* 51, no. 2 (April 1986): 273–286.

———. *Talk of Love: How Culture Matters*. Chicago, IL: University of Chicago Press, 2003.

Tamney, Joseph B. *The Resilience of Christianity in the Modern World*. Albany, NY: State University of New York Press, 1992.

Taylor, Charles. *A Secular Age*. Cambridge, MA: The Belknap Press of Harvard University Press, 2007.

Thompson, Keith. "The UFO Encounter Experience as a Crisis of Transformation." In *Spiritual Emergency: When Personal Transformation Becomes a Crisis*, edited by Stanislav Grof and Christina Grof. New York: Jeremy P. Tarcher/Putnam, 1989, pp. 121–134.

Tipton, Steven M. *Getting Saved from the Sixties: Moral Meaning in Conversion and Cultural Change*. Berkeley: University of California Press, 1984.

Troeltsch, Ernst. *The Social Teachings of the Christian Churches*. London: George Allen & Unwin, 1931.

Tschannen, Olivier. "The Secularization Paradigm: A Systematization." *Journal for the Scientific Study of Religion* 30 (1991): 395–415.

Turner, Victor. *Blazing the Trail: Way Marks in the Exploration of Symbols*, edited by Edith Turner. Tucson: University of Arizona Press, 1992.

———. *Dramas, Fields, and Metaphors: Symbolic Action in Human Society*. Ithaca: Cornell University Press, 1974.

———. *The Forest of Symbols: Aspects of Ndembu Ritual*. Ithaca: Cornell University Press, 1967.

———. *From Ritual to Theatre: The Human Seriousness of Play*. New York: PAJ Publications, 1982.

———. *The Ritual Process: Structure and Anti-Structure*. New York: Aldine de Gruyter, 1995 [1969].

Weber, Max. *Economy and Society*, edited by Guenther Roth and Claus Wittich. Berkeley: University of California Press, 1978 [1956].

———. *The Protestant Ethic and the Spirit of Capitalism*. New York: Routledge, 1987 [1904].

———. "Science as a Vocation." In *From Max Weber: Essays in Sociology*, edited by H.H. Gerth and C. Wright Mills. New York: Oxford University Press, 1946 [1919], pp. 129–256.

Wilson, Bryan. *Contemporary Transformations of Religion*. Oxford: Oxford University Press, 1976.

———. *Religion in Secular Society*. London: C.A. Watts, 1966.

———. *Religion in Sociological Perspective*. Oxford: Oxford University Press, 1982.

Wilson, Bryan. "Secularization: The Inherited Model." In *The Sacred in a Secular Age: Toward Revision in the Scientific Study of Religion*, edited by P.E. Hammond. Berkeley: University of California Press, 1985, pp. 9–20.

Wink, Walter. *The Powers That Be: Theology for a New Millennium*. New York: Three Rivers, 1999.

Wuthnow, Robert. *Acts of Compassion: Caring for Others and Helping Ourselves*. Princeton: Princeton University Press, 1991.

———. *After Heaven: Spirituality in America since the 1950s*. Berkeley: University of California Press, 1998.

———. *Rediscovering the Sacred: Perspectives on Religion in Contemporary Society*. Grand Rapids: William B Eerdmans, 1992.

———. *The Restructuring of American Religion: Society and Faith since World War II*. Princeton: Princeton University Press, 1988.

———. *Vocabularies of Public Life*. New York: Routledge, 1991.

Yamane, David. "Secularization on Trial: In Defense of a Neosecularization Paradigm." *Journal for the Scientific Study of Religion* 36, no. 1 (1997): 109–122.

INDEX